Read His Hands, Know His Heart

READ HIS HANDS, KNOW HIS HEART

*Use the Secrets of Hand Reading
For a Better Relationship
With Your Man*

by Marion Gale

RUNNING PRESS
PHILADELPHIA · LONDON

CONTENTS

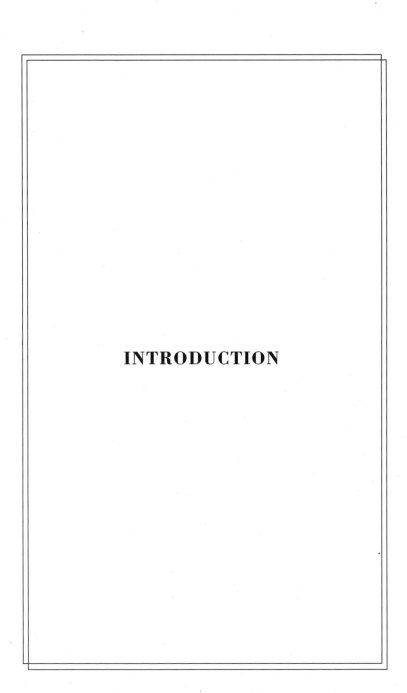

INTRODUCTION

I first had my hands read at age twenty-eight. The palmist was a suave and charming man who looked deep into my eyes and told me I was smart and strong and that I intimidated men. He said I would work in the movies one day and that I was too generous by far. All of this he could have guessed from observation. None of it helped to deal with my life or the chain of relationship disasters in it. Yet I was impressed by his reading and made a note to seek out fortune-tellers in the future.

I thought over what he'd said and concluded I needed a change. I told my young daughter, Sophie, to pack her bags for London, where I had once lived and worked. It seemed the best way to avoid more unhappy love affairs was to escape to where the grass was greener. The string of ne'er-do-wells came round to say goodbye and I thanked my lucky stars they would soon be in my past. It didn't occur to me to look inside myself for the source of my troubles. I felt that a fresh start in another country might be the answer to my prayers for a compatible partner.

The shipboard romance I sparked on our way to England reflected in every way what I had just escaped; he was a man with a troubled past but very deep green eyes and the blackest hair this side of Malta. It was typical of me to let my hormones do the thinking and put the brain on hold. I never stopped to question what *falling in love* was about, thinking that Mother Nature must have a method to her madness and would shortly let me in on the secret.

The next year passed in a blur. My career steamed ahead but

at every low point in my love life I consulted a fortune-teller. One rainy Saturday in London I visited an office on Bayswater Road and held out my hands for yet another version of "you'll be traveling over water, into the arms of a tall, dark stranger with the initial R". But this was different: I had stumbled upon Scientific Hand Analysis.

What I got was a one-hour, in-depth description of my childhood, parents, and personality, as well as my talents and abilities, all of it accurate. The hand analyst didn't stop there. For every aspect of my character that he described, he explained whether it was inherited or if it sprang from life experience.

PUTTING IT ALL TOGETHER

This reading so intrigued me that I spent the next fifteen years studying hand analysis. I took handprints and followed the lives of hundreds of people, observing how character shaped their destiny and how they influenced what happened by their own efforts. I established a private practice that specialized in compatibility readings for couples. My background as a social worker and counselor contributed to an understanding of relationships and human behavior. Eventually I combined this with hand analysis to guide people to make better choices in life, especially in close personal relationships. When I ask a client if she has any questions, I know that her answer will be, "Will I find my true love?" This book gets right to the heart of what I have learned and explains how I answer this question.

What you'll be learning in this book is how to choose a man wisely, accept him and then deal with all the normal crises that arise when two people who love each other live together. It was written so that men and women can make more informed choices about who they choose to love. *Read His Hands, Know His Heart*, along with the accompanying card deck, can help you put this together and then keep it strong.

I've read hands on planes, trains and buses, at cafes, on park benches and movie sets, at conventions, political meetings, in theatres, waiting rooms and clubs. Whenever someone put out their hand and asked me to take a look, I was ready, willing and able. What most people ask me about is contained in the card deck you'll find in this kit.

─────────

USE THE CARDS WITH CONFIDENCE

Reading a man's hands can tell you more about a potential partner in five minutes than you might learn in a year of casual dates. Remember, men can lie, but their hands do not.

Whether you're married, single, deeply in love or about to give up on a relationship, *Read His Hands, Know His Heart* has something for you. When you've finished *Read His Hands, Know His Heart*, you'll be ready to use the cards with confidence. You simply ask your man to hold up his writing hand while you go through the deck. When you find a card that matches a feature in his hand, put it aside. It doesn't have to be an exact match, but a close one. You will end up with anywhere from 12-25 cards for a reading, since every hand is uniquely different. When you turn these over, you will find a clear assessment of his character and behavior.

The flip side of the cards is designed to jog your memory on the book's details.

As you read each chapter of the book, you'll understand another layer of your man's character and the influences that have shaped him. It provides you with the insight to make your relationship strong and lasting, filled with moments of real joy. I am very excited to be able to share these secrets with you and hope that, in seeing your man up close in a whole new light, you'll find yourself falling in love with him all over again.

A WORD ABOUT THE PASSIVE HAND

To do a thorough hand analysis you should read both hands. The hand that he writes with, the dominant hand, reflects his adult character. It is believed that the passive hand reflects his childhood character and his unconscious mind. Everything that was said and done to him since he was born lives on in some manner in his unconscious. So it's possible to take a peek into that world by reading his passive hand.

Read it just the same way you read his dominant hand, except that everything that you see reflects the person he was in his childhood. In this way, you can compare it with his dominant hand and see the changes in his personality or the many things that he has overcome. Of course, some people show little difference between their passive and dominant hands.

Knowledge of what's in his passive hand is important because it explains his "alter ego". This is the person he becomes when he's been drinking or taking drugs, or if he's under a terrific pressure and can't think straight. At these times there's a chance that he will behave quite differently from the man you thought you knew and loved. Don't feel afraid. It comes from his past memories in his unconscious mind. These are a part of him but, for most of the time, they remain buried.

This chapter has provided knowledge of your man's inner emotional life and even his past, for your information. On the whole, men are reluctant to talk about such matters. They prefer to act rather than to display or speak about their feelings. Now you will be able to gauge his emotions without having to ask. Society still prefers a male who is in control at all times, who is independent and a strong achiever. In order for him to lower this mask and allow you to share his vulnerable side, he must trust you completely. You have actually seen him with his mask down when you read his hands. What you learned can put you in a place of strength to gain his trust and retain his love.

THINGS TO REMEMBER WHEN
READING HANDS

Before we get to the juicy details that contribute to his loving
ways, let's look at some things to remember when reading
hands. Most of them are common sense and worth looking at for
anyone who is new to hand analysis. When you first look at the
cards in The Love Deck, you'll see things like The Loop
of Good Humor and The Teacher's Square. Many people
jump up and say, "I've got a great sense of humor! Let's look
for my loop!" or "My friend's a professor! Where's his
Teacher's Square?"

This is an understandable and common reaction. You're very
excited to find out that the hands hold a wealth of information
and you'd like to start finding all the features. So you look in a
person's hands to see if he's got the features that denote the
character traits you see in him. But this is not the way it necessarily works.

Every person is born with different talents and abilities, as
well as his own temperament that helps shape his personality.
But more important, we are each born with a will. As we grow
up, we are given choices in life, different roads to take.
Sometimes our character decides those roads, and sometimes
our talent is just so huge that it takes us there all by itself. But
for most people, life is a continual set of challenges and decisions, and we use our smarts and our willpower to leap each
hurdle as best we can to reach our goals.

We are all actors, to some degree. Many of us put on a different persona depending on whom we are with. If it's family or close friends, we are at our most natural. But in other circumstances, like a job interview or meeting a new guy at a party, we try to let our best characteristics shine. To make an impression, we might attempt to be funny or sexy when in fact we are quite shy and subdued. Keeping up such an act is a strain. Eventually our true colors show through when the pout turns into a lop-sided grin and the jokes fall flat. These *true colors* are the character that is reflected in our hands.

Here's a mistake not to make. Let's say you're snuggled up to him on a third date and you've decided it's time to read his hands. As you look at the illustration on each card, don't try to make his hands fit what you see. For example, if you're looking at the Curved Heart Line card, don't try to turn his hand so that his heart line appears to curve. And don't ask him to splay his fingers in order to match the card with that feature. It's of the utmost importance that his hands are in a *natural* position when you match them with a card. You could ask him to shake his hand a few times before you look at it and this way it will fall into a position that is comfortable which gives an accurate reading.

I designed the backs of the cards to express the most positive aspects of each feature. This should smooth the way as you read each card. I hope that his face lights up with recognition and pride. Later, with his cards in hand, you can refer them back to the book to get more in-depth information on what they mean.

Never take just one aspect of your man and think that this

alone defines him. You need to read all the cards and then put the information together. It's part of the exciting challenge of reading hands to learn to examine all the qualities in order to see the whole person. And now we're ready to look at more features that contribute to his romantic and emotional behavior...

—*Marion Gale*

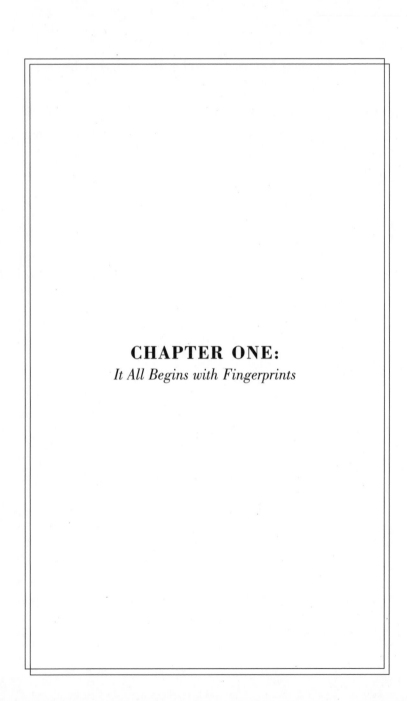

CHAPTER ONE:

It All Begins with Fingerprints

I n this book you'll learn how to get a man's hormones pumping. More important, you'll find out how to keep his love forever. You'll be let in on the secrets to his heart he may not be aware of, or he would rather not reveal. When you see how easy it is to read a man like a book you'll never look at men the same way again. In *Read His Hands, Know His Heart* I detail important elements of a man's character to compare with your own. When you're looking for a marriage partner, look for someone with both similar and compatible features. Sharp differences are exciting in the short term, but for long-term commitment and contentment, it is shared ideas, goals and values that make getting over the big hurdles possible.

I explain why you're attracted to certain men and the likely result of those unions. By the end of the book you'll be able to scan a hand quickly, even in a smoky bar or from a photo. You'll pick up secrets about men that will put you at an advantage when dealing with them. The book will help you understand the man you love and guide you when things get stormy.

When you meet a new guy, check out his physical appearance including his body language, his tone and manner of speech. The eyes tell a great deal about a man, as does his smile. When all of the usual signals have been gauged, look at his hands to confirm what you're feeling. There may be surprises. The vast majority of human beings are good people who want to love and be loved. Most of what you find in his hands will be positive and insightful. All of it will help you in your dealings with him.

For anyone who may be afraid of what's in the hands, let me

put your mind at rest. Are you nervous about a personality test? That's what hands reflect, the character you were born with and the personality you forged in order to cope with life. The lines can and do change. Your fingerprints do not. We are all born with rubbery hands, whose eventual form is influenced by how we handled childhood.

When you first fall in love, you can't get enough of each other. Then time and the daily grind put a damper on the euphoria. A man who feels rejected by his wife doesn't seek out a mistress for sex. He does it because the other woman's attention strokes his ego and this causes the brain to spike his body chemistry. The sex may be fine, but it is secondary to the massage of his ego. Men are born with a need to be seen as a winner, and that's what makes them feel good.

If you think what I'm saying is outdated, think again. I've come to these conclusions after twenty-five years of studying the lives of hundreds of couples.

Here's an illustration: On a TV dating show, a handsome Harvard graduate named Alex was asked to choose a future wife from twenty-five gorgeous women. The cameras followed him week-by-week as he interacted with, and then disposed of, all but three of the contestants. Viewers could only wonder, "Why did he choose these and not the others?"

Two of the finalists, Trista and Amanda, were blonde and buxom with beautiful smiles. Each had the ability to gaze upon Alex as though he were an Adonis and listen to him with rapt attention. They had little problem expressing their sensuality in front of the cameras while Alex had no problem lapping it up.

The third finalist, a feisty brunette who didn't smile nearly as much as the blondes, was knocked out of the competition when she took Alex home to her parents but paid more attention to her dog than she did to the bachelor. She then rebuked him in public, in the limo with the cameras rolling, when he asked a question about her attitude to sex. She spoke her mind clearly and let him know he'd been rude. Alex turned redder than the roses he'd been handing out to his chosen females. He looked humiliated and quite uncomfortable.

Media columnists fell over themselves in an attempt to analyze his final choice, the adoring Amanda. They almost universally panned the show and declared that it had demeaned women. But in fact, this show was an amazing insight into how the so-called weaker sex goes after and gets her man when she knows how to push the right buttons.

What viewers saw when Alex pared down these women was not the working of his Harvard-trained mind, but the results of the messages sent by his body chemistry to his brain. Psychologists have found that every day of his life, a man's testosterone and serotonin levels can spike or dive, according to whether he wins or loses. You could call testosterone *the sexy hormone* and serotonin *the happy hormone*.

This yo-yo effect is particularly connected to a man's interactions with other people. Please read the words over the following until they're burned into your brain: *All men want to feel sexy and happy*, and their ability to do so depends on *what is said to them*. This is a vital key to getting along with any man, and that is what Trista and Amanda did for Alex, more than any of the other contestants. These young women triggered deep-seated memories of his doting parents, a sure-fire way to get a man's attention. They were also worshipful, nurturing, agreeable and sexually available.

Is it a surprise that he chose the curvaceous blonde Amanda instead of the brunette who had the moxie to confront him in the limo? There was not a great deal of spunk to Amanda but her trump card was that she reflected Alex at twice his normal size. He said it all when he looked at the camera and expressed how he felt about her, "She makes me feel good." He's speaking about his own hormonal surges, though he doesn't know it, and this convivial young woman figured out how to trigger them.

How do you know when you've found your soul mate? Is it the adrenaline rush when you see him or the way you feel so light and bubbly when they play your song? How about the crunch in your stomach when you see him with another girl, or the loss of appetite when he doesn't call for days? It is all of these and more.

These chemical reactions occur when we're emotionally tied to another person. We're as vulnerable as a small child. This is because we're attracted to a partner who reawakens in us the most powerful memories of our parents. The reason why we suffer both joy and sorrow is because our attraction to a mate is activated in our primitive or unconscious brain, the one that is hidden from the conscious part. We search out a partner who brings back our links to childhood in order to repair the emotional damage from that time. To put it simply, we want to get another crack at daddy (or mommy) to try to make them really love us this time.

If you are lucky enough to have had stable, committed and
loving parents, your chance of repeating their successful marriage is good. For most of us, however, life wasn't like that. We
strove to overcome personality conflicts with one or both parents, or with our siblings, and may have had a less than loving
atmosphere in the home. We carry these memories in our
unconscious brain for a lifetime. They sleep peacefully most of
the time, but come awake when we see that tall, handsome guy
who turns us to jelly. Once you've learned to read hands, you'll
have a better idea of whether a marriage to him would work out
any better than your relationship with daddy (or mommy).

HIS FINGERPRINTS ARE KEY

It's one thing to be attracted to a guy, and another thing to make
the bond between you strong and lasting. This book guides you
to a new understanding of your close personal relationships and
helps you make them work long-term. Though it is specifically
aimed at women to read the character of their men, the information can also be applied to friends and family members, as well
as the reader herself. We start with the most important aspect of
the personality because it's written in stone—the fingerprints.

While it's not necessary for soul mates to share exact fingerprint types, it's important that your print patterns be compatible
with his. To know a man's fingerprints is to have a good grasp of
his basic behavior and inner drives. There are three main fin-

gerprint patterns: the Loop, the Whorl and the Arch. Each reflects the distinct character traits of its owner. Many people have different prints on one hand. Look at the print on the Index Finger of the hand he writes with, his dominant hand. This print is the most important because it's on the finger that represents his ego.

Look at the way people use their hands and fingers. What other digit gets as much use as the index finger? We point with it, gesture with it, stroke it with our thumbs when we're agitated, stick it into holes and crevices, pick up coins with it, rub our eyes and poke holes with it, guide our pens and chopsticks with this finger, explore our lover's body, and more. It is the most direct servant of our brain, of all our exterior body parts.

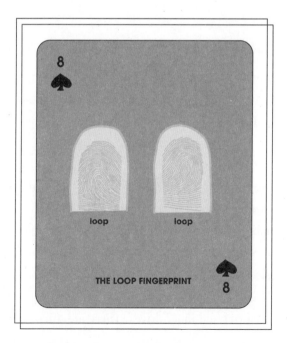

THE LOOP FINGERPRINT

THE LOOP PERSONALITY *(I FIT IN)*

The man with a Loop Fingerprint *(8 of Spades)* on his index finger is easygoing, popular and adaptable. He can take on any work and make a go of it. His workmates respond to him as a good buddy. If he finds himself in a crisis, he'll pull together a group to work out the problems. He's an all-round, well-balanced, and capable guy. This is rarely a man with hard edges, unless he had a particularly brutal childhood. Because he's flexible and capable, he can deal with upsets and then put them in his past.

The Loop man will be a welcome member on any team. He'll also be popular on a committee, tending to tread the middle ground. He's a great host at a party and mixes well with every kind of guest. It's a good idea for him to take up hobbies or join a gym because the Loop is the most prone to become a couch potato. For him, it's wise to seek out stimulation because it doesn't come from within him. He can marry any fingerprint type and accommodate their differences.

The Loop person gets along with all the other fingerprint types.

THE WHORL PERSONALITY *(I THINK)*

The man with a Whorl fingerprint *(6 of Spades)* on his index finger is the individualist and thinker who has an artistic or creative nature found with the Whorl person. Because he spends a great deal of time in his own private world, thinking, reading, and dreaming, he will have clearly formed opinions. A Whorl person is thoughtful, intense, and self-contained. He has an innately private nature and does not reveal his personal feelings easily or willingly.

The Whorl person enjoys solitude but can empathize and easily bond with other Whorls, as well as those from the Whorl family; The Peacock's Eye, and the Composite. He can get along with a Loop person, as does everyone. He is at opposite ends of the spectrum from an Arch, however. If you marry a Whorl, it's a good idea to accept that his need to keep hidden many personal feelings is of the utmost importance to him. He is not shutting you out, but rather protecting his own strong need for privacy and the inner world that is his creation and his refuge.

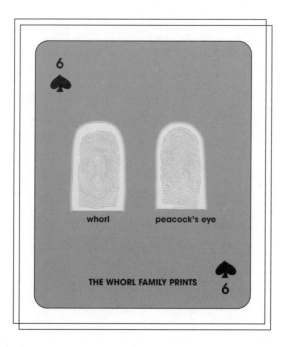

whorl   peacock's eye

THE WHORL FAMILY PRINTS

THE ARCH PERSONALITY *(I Do)*

The man with an Arch fingerprint *(7 of Spades)* on his index finger is practical, efficient, reliable and hardworking. He's reserved and prefers to keep his emotions under wraps. If there's a repair to be done, a manual to follow, or a map to be read, the Arch fingerprint is your guy. He's suspicious and doesn't believe anything until it's been proved. In an emergency, he's Mr. Unflappable who solves the problem calmly and with common sense. In a changing world, he'll be the last to accept innovation. If you're planning a move, give him plenty of time to get used to the idea and remember that he'll want good reasons for it.

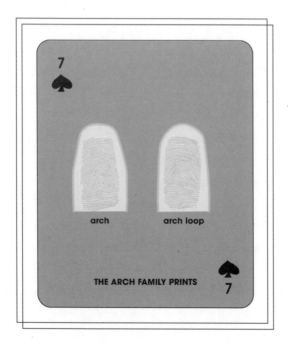

arch   arch loop

THE ARCH FAMILY PRINTS

The Arch person can get along easily with a Loop or another Arch person. And while they can adapt to a Whorl, simply because being practical is what they're all about, there isn't a great deal of common ground for these very different personalities. However, when love is strong, and particularly if a couple is mature, it can make an interesting combination. As a romantic partner, the Arch fingerprint person appears to be the least demonstrative and doesn't often smile or jump for joy on the outside, but can feel intensely on the inside.

OTHER COMMON PRINTS

VARIATIONS ON THE WHORL FINGERPRINT

The Peacock's Eye *(6 of Spades)* is technically half Loop and half Whorl but the traits of a Whorl are more intense than those of a Loop. So if he has a Peacock's Eye on his index finger, read the Whorl card. People with a Peacock's Eye have a specific artistic sensibility, such as an eye for design and color or a love of music, as well as sharing the basic characteristics of the Whorl personality. How intense these traits are will depend on the other prints on the remaining fingers.

The Composite *(9 of Spades)* fingerprint pattern also belongs to the Whorl family but I gave it its own card because of its special features. The owner of a Composite print shares the traits of a Whorl, plus a lot more. They have a need for variety, have a difficult time making up their mind on anything and then are apt to change it again suddenly. Being able to see two sides to

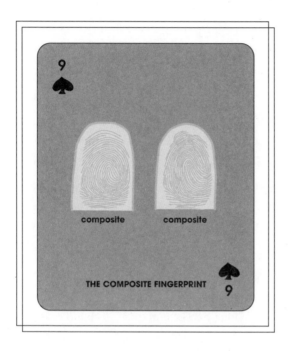

every issue means they make good mediators. Composite fingerprint people can change their name or address at the drop of a hat. They have a talent for doing more than two things at once. They'll probably have many careers during their lifetime and perform each one with the same enthusiastic intensity. There's never a dull moment with a Composite print person in the family!

Of the three fingerprint types, Loop, Arch, and Whorl, it is particularly the Whorl person who is attracted to other Whorls or its family members, the Composite and Peacock's Eye. Loops can get along with anyone and the Arch can make do with any other print because of their practical nature. But the Whorl person feels a particularly strong bond with those from the Whorl family. And there is no doubt that their close personal relationships with each other have a special intensity and passion.

VARIATION ON THE ARCH FINGERPRINT

The Arch-Loop *(7 of Spades)* is a Loop that lies so low that it has almost flattened out to look like an Arch. This is a fascinating combination of the easygoing Loop with the practical Arch fingerprint. This guy will be a low-key but sociable type and always handy around the house. He's got manual dexterity and likes to feel useful. He's a good problem-solver, like the pure Arch, so he'll be thrilled to help you with your taxes, share puzzles, figure out maps and manuals, as well as keep the yard looking great. Don't expect him to be wild and crazy but he can be just as loving, in his own calm way, as the poetic Whorl. He just doesn't go in for outward displays of emotion and tends to speak in a direct manner, getting to the point.

If you take a look at the fingerprints of the people you feel closest to, you'll find that many of them have prints similar to your own. We seek out people with whom we have things in common, not just for marriage but for friendships as well. In the next chapter we're going to check out real-life couples, their fingerprints, and how their romantic relationships fared. You will have a whole new view of the world, of yourself, your family members and, most important, of your boyfriend. Always remember — to know him, really know him, is to understand and love him, more than you ever thought possible.

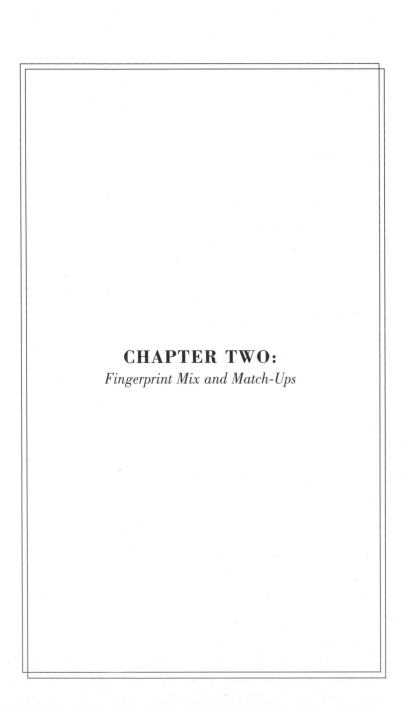

CHAPTER TWO:

Fingerprint Mix and Match-Ups

L et's look at real-life case histories, concentrating on the compatibility of their fingerprint patterns. By getting to know the characteristics that accompany each print, you can get to the core of his behavior and stay one jump ahead of him. Also, you can decide which type is for you. Spending a lifetime with someone takes a great deal of patience and fortitude. Before you invest any precious time, be sure of what you are getting into. The traits reflected in a fingerprint overlap all of his other features.

THE LOOP WITH THE WHORL

Debbie had been through the mill with more men than she could count, including two husbands whose photos no longer graced her albums. She was a savvy career woman who took the top prize for sales year after year. Customers loved her, and sweet persuasion plus a hearty laugh were her ways to their hearts, not the high-pressure routines used by many co-workers. If her professional life was a success, her personal life went entirely in the other direction.

When I looked at her hands, I saw a well-balanced and stable individual. Her fingers were straight and strong. But the key to her personality was the Loop Fingerprint on her index finger plus Loops on many other fingers as well. I knew she was doing her best to make her marriage to Mark work. The Loop is the sign of a well-balanced person who fits in with others. They tend to be easygoing and good at dealing with difficult people or sticky situations. You don't get a strident character with the Loop fingerprint. What you get is the sort of person who is voted most popular.

Since Loop people are also flexible and capable, it wasn't for want of trying that Debbie's marriage was a mess. When I printed her husband's hands, they showed an almost full set of Whorl prints, including his index fingers. Our index finger is the digit that represents our ego. That's why it's of the utmost importance when reading a person's hands.

Your fingerprints never change. The Whorl personality is probably the most misunderstood. Whorl people are thoughtful, creative, intense, enthusiastic and secretive. They commonly have an artistic nature. Because they tend to be introspective, they can become very wrapped up in their own world. They're not the easiest people to live with if you're a sociable Loop person like Debbie. She just couldn't understand why her husband was reluctant to party or chat up a storm like she could with anyone who walked in her door. It's a matter of personal comfort level.

When you're dating a man with Whorl fingerprints, especially if he has plenty of them, he'll be intense, moody and mysterious, all very sexy and fascinating. But once you're married, he doesn't just pop out of his shell. That shell is the real him and he needs it to protect his privacy. You cannot pry him open like a clam but must respect his solitary nature. Just because he doesn't babble away doesn't mean he isn't thinking about you. It's just not his nature to be open about his personal thoughts and feelings.

Ask him his opinion on politics or world affairs, inquire about his hobbies, and you'll get an enthusiastic reply. Whorls tend to look deeply into things and to think a great deal, so they have very definite opinions. If he's got a Long Head Line, he could even talk the hind leg off a horse. Just don't pry into his personal affairs. That's the compartment he keeps closed for his own deep-seated reasons. I always make it a point to tell parents who have a Whorl child to give him a diary and encourage him to fill it. What he can't share with another person he can often pour into written words. It provides an outlet for his childhood angst.

If you find yourself in love with a man with many Whorl fingerprints, especially on the index fingers, learn to appreciate his uniqueness and creativity. This is not the sort of guy who can go on a talk show and spill his guts in front of the world. That is the territory of the other fingerprint types. Whorls are intense and introspective and full of opinions when probed gently. It must be apparent by now why Debbie and Mark were not getting along after five years and two kids. She was popular and loved to socialize, with her lovely Loops allowing her to relax and enjoy all kinds of different people; he was quiet and introspective, compulsively collecting science fiction, lost in his own world as only a Whorl person can be.

Both felt isolation within the marriage. Whorl people like Mark tend to think a great deal and try to figure out such things as "why are we all here in the first place?" He needed to bounce these ideas off someone once in a while, but Debbie was content to discuss the Key Lime pie recipe she'd stumbled onto, or how the new neighbors were shaping up. The deep, dark and intense inner world of her husband was not of any real interest to her.

Mark was an individualist, while Debbie was happy being sociable. He was not comfortable at the parties she loved to throw and she didn't understand why he stood against the wall, unable to talk freely with their guests until he'd downed a few beers. Once he got onto a subject, however, he was Mister Fascination and other women could be charmed by his intensity and knowledge and his brooding good looks.

Could this marriage have been saved? It is true that a Loop Fingerprint person like Debbie can get along with any of the other fingerprint types. That is their great strength. But to live at close quarters with someone so different, and raise children together, can be a tall order. In fact, this marriage could have gone on for longer if they'd had other things in common. A shared sense of humor, for example, could have helped them through the rough spots.

Four years after their divorce, Debbie was sunning on a beach in Florida, enjoying the warm, fresh air and keeping a keen eye on her boys. She noticed a man checking her out. He'd pry his nose out of his book from time to time and take a gander at the still-seductive single mother. His children frolicked nearby. Before the day was out, Debbie drew on her Loop affability and went over to introduce herself to the attractive man, whose name was Bob. They've now been married twenty years, and it's been pretty smooth sailing. Like Debbie, Bob is a Loop person. Their social world is a focal point of their lives and everyone loves to attend their flamboyant parties with Bob at the piano and Debbie singing up a storm.

A Loop person can fall in love with the highly individualistic Whorl personality. Understanding their nature as described in this book will help greatly. It will be emotional differences that most often arise between them. The Whorl can also be attracted to the calm and sociable Loop, who has an all-round capable nature.

The Loop is easygoing while the Whorl is intense and has a rich and private inner world. The Whorl is more likely to be an artist, while the Loop is content to attend the gallery where her Whorl partner's art is on display. Each partner in this pair has something special to contribute to a successful marriage, but must be willing to accept their emotional differences.

When a Loop teams up with another Loop, given that they have other features in common in their hands, there is going to be a strong bond and a lively social life.

They'll feel at ease with each other in every situation and cope with life well as a team.

THE LOOP WITH THE ARCH

Julia grew up next door to Todd and they were fast friends all through high school. She had the Arch fingerprint pattern and her character reflected all its traits. She was reliable, practical, self-sufficient and in control of her emotions. There was a lot of family strife in both teenagers' homes and they clung to one another for support. Todd came to depend on Julia's cool head and quick solutions to any problem that arose. She was the sort of woman that you'd want on board your ship, should it be sinking fast.

Todd was a very popular guy, voted Mr. Congeniality at the Senior Prom. He was always there to help a friend and had a way with one-liners that put people at ease and made them like him. His Loop fingerprints were a boon for dealing with his difficult family. They reflected his even-tempered nature, which kept him steady during times of conflict. He loved his parents and never told them how much their constant bickering upset him.

So Julia and Todd were drawn to each other, but it was not white-hot lust or even romantic love. For her, he was an attractive young man who made her laugh and seemed to care about her troubles. He was always there with a shoulder to cry on. To him, Julia was the steady source of moral support and practical advice. They both felt that the other supplied something that they lacked or needed. And so they drifted into a more intimate relationship and, finally, they married.

Julia's pragmatic nature prodded her to make the marital decisions and Todd was content to go along with them. She postponed having a family because she wanted to get her University degree. This meant they had many years with just the two of them and a whole 24 hours a day to fill. Todd, the affable Loop guy, always complied with his wife's wishes. If she wanted to shop for garden supplies, he drove her to the nursery and helped her fill the car with seedlings. If she decided to take up karate, he stayed home with the dog every Tuesday night until she returned.

It never occurred to Todd that Julia was looking for something outside of the marriage. But she found it unexpectedly in her karate instructor. As the lessons got later and later, it still didn't click with Todd that his competent, dependable Julia could be going into overtime for more than a Black Belt. What had happened was this: Julia had married Todd in haste, before she tasted life to the full. Her practical nature told her she might be missing out on something, that there could be more to life than a husband who does everything you ask, with pleasure. So when Mr. Exciting came into view, she decided to test other waters. She did not fall in love with her new lover. An Arch person approaches everything in a calm and deliberate fashion.

She told Todd she thought they should separate. Now the many signs and signals he had chosen to ignore all added up. He realized what was going on and felt the need to blow his top. Julia kept her cool, but he ranted and raved about how she'd shamed him, after all he'd done for her, and he didn't see any need to carry on the marriage. Like Mark and Debbie, this couple ended up in the divorce courts. Maybe they should have taken time to work things out.

Twenty years after the divorce, I met them both on separate occasions. Julia had remarried and Todd was living with his long-time girlfriend. But both confided in me that they'd never found the same compatibility that they'd enjoyed when they were together. As Julia said, "When you're young, the hormones take over. You think that great sex is necessary for a strong relationship. But you have to talk with that man in the morning. And then you get older and suddenly realize that the comfortable companionship you had in the marriage was just as important as great sex, if not more so. But we wise up too late. It was over and done with so long ago." Todd echoed her sentiments.

What you have with the Loop and Arch fingerprint couple is a steady and well-balanced pair who can face life's struggles and build a solid life together. It's probably a good combination for raising a family. If Julia and Todd had produced children, chances are it would have been a richly rewarding experience that could have cemented the marriage. Todd would have been the lovable dad while Julia concentrated on discipline and order and used her skills to cook up delectable meals for their hungry brood. The differences between a Loop and an Arch are not as extreme as the differences between either of them and a member of the Whorl family.

THE WHORL WITH THE ARCH

You've read descriptions of the Arch and Whorl patterns. It might seem that to match these two personality types would be a disaster: the intense, thoughtful Whorl with the practical, suspicious Arch. And you might be correct. But like everything connected to human nature, we can overcome great obstacles where there's a will. This is the only match that requires two descriptions. When the woman has a Whorl print and the man has an Arch, and then the other way around. The reason for this is because the Arch fingerprint traits are traditionally considered to be "masculine." And so when a woman has Arch fingerprints, she goes through life with an extra burden because she is often judged to be cold and/or calculating when the truth is that she is simply practical, not inclined to approach issues from an emotional angle.

THE WHORL FEMALE
WITH THE ARCH MALE

Rob was born with Arches on his index fingers and sprinkled across others as well. He liked sports as a boy and took up sailing and rock climbing. Building things with his hands seemed to come naturally. He was widely admired by the younger kids because of his cool and calm approach. If there was trouble in the neighborhood, they turned to Rob to drive away bullies or solve the problem, which he always did. He went into the military for a while and then left to start up his own construction business.

He didn't marry young like many of his pals, but held out for that very special girl. She came along just before he turned thirty and he was as smitten as any man could be. Lynn was young, beautiful and brilliant, everything he thought he wanted in a woman. She had Whorl fingerprints on her index fingers and elsewhere. Lynn was lively and intelligent, so for some time Rob didn't notice that she never discussed anything personal. They married shortly after meeting, in the heat of the moment.

In the eyes of friends and family, it was the perfect marriage. The successful builder took up with a creative and smart partner who could run his home to perfection. And she did just that. But within a year of marrying, this pair came to realize just how different their natures were. Rob was the voice of reason while Lynn flew into emotional storms, often due to his apparent *lack* of emotional response. Nobody is more intense than the Whorl personality or more prone to erratic emotions. Unfortunately, the Arch is the one fingerprint type that can push them over the edge, due to sheer frustration at what the Whorl perceives as a lack of response when a situation calls for it. The truth is that an Arch person can be steaming up plenty on the inside but he just doesn't show it on the outside. Yet people, especially an excitable Whorl, tend to read his cool outward appearance and jump to conclusions.

While Lynn kept the home spotless, her heart was not in the tasks at hand. She always had a book or magazine in one hand and a reluctant dishcloth in the other. The Whorl person is an individualist with ideas and opinions. Rob was more of a practical type, content to light his pipe after a hard day's work and let world affairs settle themselves while he popped a beer and chuckled over endless sitcom reruns.

Lynn thought she had solved the marital discord when she began to have the first of their six children. This settled things for awhile. The kids were livewires who kept them so busy they almost forgot about their differences. That is, until it came time for discipline. Lynn was so distraught over the problems that led to each crisis that she couldn't think straight. Inevitably, Rob would get out the belt and settle everything quickly, once and for all. Tears would flow, Lynn's as much as her children's, and Rob would try to make it up by taking everyone out on a picnic.

The outings only intensified the situation. While the kids screamed out for a stop in the woods and a romp in the sun, Rob aimed the car for Point B and drove relentlessly. Even pit stops for ice cream caused a ruckus. Rob kept a tight grip on family finances, with his practical nature, and thought Lynn should have packed a snack for their brood. The oldest girl sat like the calm in the eye of the storm, while the younger ones spun circles around her. She was the only child who had inherited their father's Arch fingerprints.

There were good days and bad. Lynn's creative nature gave the children a great deal of joy while their father's cool demeanor kept a lid on the worst upsets. This couple compromised for the sake of the children, which was a very mature approach to a sticky situation. As for their personal lives, Lynn and Rob came to accept that they were completely different and that's all there was to it.

Lynn would sometimes daydream about what might have been—but she gave, and got, great happiness from her children. Rob sometimes thought back to the simple girls he'd passed up for Lynn, but was thankful for the wonderful mother he'd gained for his kids. They both thought, "What the heck can you do but tough it out until the chicks have flown the coop?" Which is exactly what they did.

When the last child went off to college, Lynn quietly filed for divorce. Rob was taken by surprise. He figured they'd just stick it out. After all, they'd been together so many years, why not go the whole nine yards? But his wife had other plans. She still had energy and enthusiasm for life and wanted to enjoy her twilight years to the full, with books, theater and the cinema. Rob wouldn't do so well out on his own. Like many men, he needed an anchor. But Lynn was out the door so fast he never saw her dust.

THE WHORL MALE
WITH THE ARCH FEMALE

Michael met Jenny at a social justice meeting. He was impressed by her quick mind and by her ability to speak out on any issue with common sense, something that her full set of Arch fingerprints made easy. She had raven hair and a great figure, and she wasn't shy about showing it off. Michael thought about her a lot and finally asked her out. They had a lot in common and were soon an item. Jenny suggested he move into her big house so they could share the expenses. It seemed like a good idea at the time to Michael, who had fallen head over heels for this goddess. She felt she had a good catch in the young lawyer. His Whorl fingerprints gave him a smoldering and intense personality. Jenny always felt there was plenty hidden beneath his bright exterior and she looked forward to delving into his private world.

As the years passed by, Michael did indeed move onward and upward in his career, but not quite the way Jenny had hoped.

Because he had a big heart and had always championed the underdog, Michael found himself taking on cases *pro bono* for those too poor to afford a lawyer. And when he wasn't away at court, he loved to delve into New Age books about reincarnation and the meaning of life. Jenny watched all of this with a sense of shock, and often caved in to her rising anxiety about his lack of interest in making money. She nagged him, pointing out with a great degree of accuracy that he would "never amount to anything" if he didn't go for the blue-chip clientele. When the nagging didn't work, she would throw dishes, just missing him by inches.

Michael felt that if Jenny had a child she could focus her energies away from him and into a more practical vocation as mother. But Jenny had no intention of having children. Oh, hadn't they discussed that when they were dating? Michael was a bit of a dreamer and had just assumed that Jenny would want to raise a family with him. But as time went by and his salary barely rose, Jenny was pounding the digits on her calculator and had figured out that having kids would deplete their supply of fine wine and cut back drastically on theatre outings. This she was not prepared to do.

In fact, it was their generous amount of disposable income that kept under wraps just how at odds these two people actually were. They were able to enjoy restaurants and vacations thanks to Jenny's private income. Though they both loved this cultural buffet, the fact is that it acted like a buffer in their marriage, ensuring that they never really had time alone to think and talk. Jenny had given up on ever finding out any deep, dark inner secrets that Michael may have been hiding from her. He simply didn't like to talk about personal issues.

And while Jenny had no problem spilling the beans about her own traumatic childhood, she could see that Michael was uneasy listening to her stories and could not give her any follow-up love and reassurance. They did share some wonderful times, especially when they had artist friends over and could shine as host and hostess. Jenny was a superb cook. Michael was always at the center of any discussion on what was new in the avant garde. But when the crowd had gone and Michael was still talking about the ideas that had poured out during a lively discussion, Jenny would insist he get to work with a dishtowel and clean up their guests' mess right away. You could say that Jenny drained away all of Michael's enthusiasm.

Then one day he met a simple girl who told him just with her eyes that he was wonderful. And he lapped up her approval like a hungry dog. But it was Jenny who filed for divorce when she found out about his affair. And she took Michael to the cleaners in her divorce affidavit. Ever the pragmatist, she intended to get even for the years when she could have been married to an upwardly mobile husband rather than Michael. When I saw the four-page list of demands that she made and that Michael granted her in the divorce, I was stunned. I think he walked away with a suitcase and his dignity but not much else. Well, yes, he walked away with a smile, knowing he would never again have to answer her demands about why he didn't focus on making more money. And he married another dreamer with Whorls and lived happily ever after, while Jenny continues to search for the perfect man with an extra large bank balance.

The Arch and the Whorl couple definitely present the greatest challenge in the fingerprint world. Almost all their basic characteristics are at opposite ends of the spectrum. The unflappable, practical Arch may rarely crack a smile, unless he's got a superb Loop of Good Humor. The Arch fingerprint is not a big deal when found on a man, as it reflects traditional male traits. But if it's the female who has an Arch, especially if, like Jenny, she has that print on several fingers, she can be perceived as cool or even icy. I once saw a famous and beautiful television personality described in this rude manner, "That bitch is cold as custard." I knew she had Arch fingerprints. The calm exterior is often mistaken for callousness. An Arch female does not waste any time getting into an emotional tizzy over things. She gets everything done properly and efficiently and always has things under control.

Meanwhile, the Whorl partner is immersed in a private world of creative intensity and dreams. As long as both people have a satisfying career that makes use of their separate energies, the private life can run smoothly. But there will always be major differences between these two people. It's almost like the Arch person throws cold water onto the giddy enthusiasms that emanate from the brain of a Whorl partner. The more mature they are when they fall in love and the more intense their attraction to each other, the easier it will be to handle the differences.

OTHER COMBINATIONS

There's little need to go into great detail about Loop-Loop or Whorl-Whorl or even Arch-Arch fingerprint couples. You've just learned the character traits of each fingerprint pattern. The fact is that we get along best with those who are most like us. When you're with someone who has the same dominant print patterns as you have, there will always be a feeling that you come from the same tribe, even if you have other personality differences. In fact, if you look at the prints of your closest friends, you'll find that many of them share your index fingerprint patterns.

A couple who both have Loop patterns will get along well, have loads of friends and have a busy social life. They'll be happy to tag along with others on adventures, rather than being the instigators, and are always pleasant company. They must take care that they don't become couch potatoes. Taking up active hobbies would be a wise solution. As long as there are no major personal problems, theirs should be a very happy and compatible union.

Two Whorl print people can make a formidable creative team. The simple fact is that Whorls are attracted to other Whorls and, as the most intense of the fingerprint pattern people, they can empathize with each other. They won't have the lively social life of Mr. and Mrs. Loop, but they'll appreciate each other's need for solitude, and they'll hopefully tolerate the silences that might drive a Loop partner wild. If other aspects of their hands are compatible, they could experience some of the greatest moments of intense emotion through their shared experiences.

However, they should be aware that communication is an important way to keep things from bottling up and then boiling over. So the only warning I will give for Whorl couples is that if you both have a large number of Whorls on your fingers, you must be prepared to deal with certain behaviors in your partner, such as silent withdrawal when hurt, or complete withdrawal when concentrating on a personal project. Whorls are the obsessive-compulsives amongst us. Make every effort to let your partner know when you're feeling neglected or alone because emotional isolation can tear apart even a strong bond.

An Arch print couple is a good bet for a successful team, but it's best for them to have other features in common in their hands as well, since they are the most reluctant to change. If otherwise well matched, an Arch fingerprint couple would have a solid and stable relationship. They will be known for their practical good sense, delectable home-cooking, handyman talents, suspicious natures and calm approach to everything. They would enjoy hands-on hobbies like carpentry, archery, scuba-diving and gardening and would grow as a couple from sharing such activities.

WHAT ABOUT THE COMPOSITE? CAN *ANYBODY* LIVE WITH THEM?

The Composite fingerprint is found on a person who loves variety and who has many of the Whorl characteristics—intense, creative, and an individualist. Just try going somewhere with a Composite and see if you don't end up at a different event from the one you set out for. All you can do is draw a breath and try not to notice that the Composite didn't even blink at the turnabout.

The sociable and easy going Loop fingerprint person will find a Composite challenging and fascinating but perhaps too scatter-brained and changeable for a long-term basis such as marriage. But if the love is strong, these two can definitely make a go of things, keeping in mind their differences and learning to laugh as they go through life dealing with them.

A Whorl person feels quite at home with a Composite partner. They're both part of the Whorl family group who have such a strong feeling of a shared inner world. They also have a great deal of empathy for the solitude needed from time to time, a sort of recharging the batteries. And of course a fellow Composite print would be the most understanding of a Composite's peculiarities, which wouldn't seem peculiar to him at all, but rather deliciously familiar.

But for an Arch to be asked to live alongside a Composite— well, just take a look at what I wrote about the Arch being the most resistant to change. But a Composite person lives for change, so the one who is the more dominant partner in the marriage will take the lead while the other drags along. If the Composite partner dominates, he or she could pull up stakes and move or change jobs at the drop of a hat, while the Arch grits his teeth and sheds a silent tear. On the other hand, each day at noon, when the Arch whips up the same cheese and tomato sandwich cut exactly into quarters—and I am talking about every single day of the marriage—the Composite will look on in horror and head out the door for Chinese food. This combination has the greatest chance of ending up in the divorce courts. But if the couple is mature and understands and accepts their differences and can love each other despite them (and have otherwise compatible hands) this too can work out beautifully, but it's the longest shot.

SUMMING UP THE CHARACTERISTICS OF HIS INDEX FINGERPRINT TYPE

You can modify the traits that go with a fingerprint type, but you can never erase them completely. Most of us are happy with who we are and are accepting of our basic character. When you have read a lot of hands, you will learn that most people are fairly positive, capable and well -balanced. In other words, they are willing to work on tweaking anything they are not happy about.

There is little reason for the skyrocketing divorce rates that we see today. If a couple really wants to keep their marriage strong, the information in this book should help tremendously. To know him is to love him. To know what can be tweaked and what can't is an important first step. This chapter on fingerprints reveals an intrinsic part of the man you love. These characteristics, because they're genetic, are ingrained in his DNA and won't change.

SOME FINAL COMMENTS

What if you have looked at the fingerprint on the index finger of the man you worship and it doesn't seem to fit into any of the aforementioned groups? In other words, it is unique. When there are not enough examples of one print for us to study and apply particular behavioral patterns, it's safe to say that this print reflects a unique person. I always tell someone who has a one-off fingerprint type that after he was born, God threw away the mold, and he should be proud of his uniqueness. The truth is that oddball or eccentric personalities know they are different and most of them are thankful to be apart from the herd.

Keep in mind that the *more* fingerprints he has of the type found on his index finger, the more extremely will he fit the characteristics of that type. Conversely, if he has a sprinkling of other fingerprint patterns, especially some Loops, this alters the intensity of the index print traits. Having Loops on the other fingers waters down the intensity of a different index print. Yet that print will still define his dominant character.

What if your man has a *different* fingerprint on the Index Finger of his passive hand? Say he's got a Whorl on his left Index Finger and yet his dominant right Index Finger has a Loop. What does this mean? Since the passive hand is said to reflect our childhood and our unconscious mind, it can be important to check this print. In this case, your boyfriend would have been a more intense and private person when he was young and influenced by the Whorl print. As an adult, however, he feels freer to express himself and will have a more active social life, under the influence of his Loop print. Having the two different prints simply makes him a more complex person. He will be able to relate to, and empathize with, other people who have the Whorl, since he was once under its direct influence.

Most people have similar prints on their two index fingers. But it's always fascinating to have a glimpse of what his childhood was like if your man has a print on his passive hand that is different. And he will be amazed that you have this insight into his private world, his thoughts and feelings and attitudes, even when he was young!

Now that you are familiar with basic characteristics that will be with him for all of his life, be sure to overlap this information with what you learn about him in the following chapters. It's never wise to grab a guy and yell, "Hey! You've got Whorls so you're not going to talk much!" when it's possible that he has a Long Little Finger and a Long Head Line, both of which bestow the gift of gab. Of course, Mr. Whorl may talk at length on many subjects but he'll never spill the beans about his private life. Pull together all the elements that make up his personality before you put it all together to define him.

CHAPTER THREE:

Skin Ridges: Tiny Patterns That Pack a Punch

Y ou've had a peek at the first layer of your man's personality. Let's add another important aspect that's a
permanent part of his character. The skin ridges that
make up your fingerprints actually extend across the whole
palm. Since eighty-five percent of us have one or more of these
patterns, it's vital to understand how they reflect behavior.

Apply this information to your man with wit and wisdom, love
and empathy. What I am giving you in this book are the keys to
his character, to the sources of his pride, as well as his hidden
vulnerabilities. When you have the puzzle finally assembled, by
the end of the last chapter, you'll have a whole new view of him
built on insight and awareness.

Get out a magnifying glass or check his hands in a strong
light – sunlight is best - and you'll see the skin ridge patterns
clearly. There are four important ones. The first is a loop
between the Little Finger and the Ring Finger. This is known as
The Loop of Good Humor *(Jack of Diamonds)*. When any skin
ridge loop is on the large size, the traits are more pronounced.
Conversely, if the loop is small, the traits will come in a milder
form. But these traits will always be there, because skin ridges
are permanent.

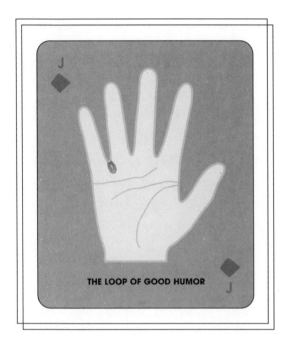

THE LOOP OF GOOD HUMOR

THE LOOP OF GOOD HUMOR
IN HIS DOMINANT HAND

Alan is only thirty-five but he's had a half dozen different jobs.
You'll recognize him by the grin on his face or mischievous
twinkle in his eye. The good-sized Loop of Good Humor in his
dominant hand reflects his carefree manner. He'll swing into the
office later than most, never miss a coffee break, and hit the
door at 5PM on the dot to get home for his wife's prize-winning
desserts. He prefers a job that he enjoys and likes to work at his
own pace. It's important for him to have congenial workmates

and a pleasant environment. After all, he's going to be there all day, every day. He likes to chew the fat with his co-workers, not because he's ingratiating himself to make his way to the top, but just because it's his nature to be easy going.

You may catch Alan with his feet up on the desk, tossing paper planes out the window. He'll be happy to organize the company picnic and even put on a dog costume in torrid heat if it makes the kids laugh. If his job gets tedious or his fellow employees get on his nerves, he'll start thinking that it's time to move on. A spotty work record doesn't faze him. Ever the optimist, he figures there's always another chance around the corner. He does not live to work, but rather works to live. Making buckets of money is way down on his list of priorities.

Alan is a genial dad, one who takes his boys out fishing or biking at the drop of a hat. Punishing them is something he'd rather leave to his wife. He'd never dream of bringing work home from the office or spending a precious family weekend putting in overtime. Landscape painting is a hobby and he's off to scope out new scenery every chance he gets. Many people admire his work and he daydreams of being self-sufficient as an artist one day.

In the meantime, good food, agreeable friends, and fun are of importance to Alan. He's a popular guy at parties, treasures his days off, and genuinely enjoys taking friends for an ice cream blowout at a favorite diner. All in all, having a Loop of Good Humor can seem like a blessing. The only drawback is you'll rarely find these men rising to the top in a dog-eat-dog business environment or picking up the Nobel Prize for Science. It doesn't bother them, so make sure it doesn't bother you.

The Loop of Good Humor can seem like a misleading name. It doesn't mean the person has a pronounced sense of humor, though some certainly do. Rather, these people have a laid-back attitude to life and so probably enjoy more laughs than most others. They're built to handle the stress and angst of everyday life just a bit more easily than other people. If the Loop is twisted to the side, it reflects a sarcastic or unusual sense of humor, like the guy you'll find dropping hilarious one-liners behind the boss's back or lobbing water balloons well into his middle-age. No doubt he'll also be the first to volunteer for early retirement.

TO SUM UP THE LOOP OF GOOD HUMOR

This guy is easygoing, not bothered by the odd spot of unemployment, able to fill his spare time with ease, likes to party, takes the time to stop and smell the roses, gets a kick out of his kids, is rarely focused on getting ahead or on making money. He can be both successful and happy in a career that employs several of these traits, such as balloon artist with *Cirque du Soleil*, a bicycle courier or the product tester for a game company. He can be good at any job that he truly enjoys doing.

Now take a look at the space between his Ring and Middle Fingers. If there's a loop here, it's known as The Loop of Serious Intent.

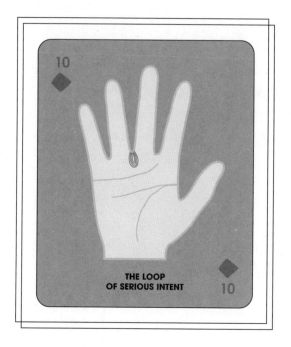

THE LOOP OF SERIOUS INTENT
IN HIS DOMINANT HAND

David looks like a laid-back bohemian but don't let that mop of hair and cherubic face fool you. He's got a medium-sized Loop of Serious Intent *(10 of Diamonds)* in his dominant hand and it reflects almost every move he makes, every thought that pops into his head. David likes to laugh just as much as the next guy. But he always held down a full-time job and has worked his way slowly up the corporate ladder.

He married a woman he fell hard for when she proved to have

a good mind as well as a great pair of legs. The marriage is important to David. He feels very much part of a couple and wants their union to be forever. Everyone seems to get the best from this man. His boss gets an employee who rarely calls in sick and performs his duties with diligence and with an eye on the prize. His wife gets a husband who pays the bills, took out a sizeable life insurance policy for her, and actually likes being a good husband.

Admittedly, there's not a load of laughs. And don't try to make light of important issues around this guy. He's aware of starving kids in Africa, the holes being punched in our ozone layer, and why gas prices are getting scary. This essentially responsible approach to life drives him to get to the bottom of things. He may even try to change the world. David's the first to give to charity at the office and the last to turn out the lights when a job calls for overtime.

David tends to be a worrywart. He's lucky he married a woman who's mature, perceptive and caring. Their hands have a great deal in common, so much so that they often communicate without speaking. The fact that their marriage is a haven gives him respite from most anxiety when he's home. You'll be reading about another feature that exacerbates worrying in a later chapter. If your man has several indications that reflect an anxious approach to life, it's a clue for you to be supportive and nurturing and to be a rock for him. Occasionally you'll find a guy with the Loop of Serious Intent who appears to be a jokester, but watch him carefully and you'll see there's nothing lightweight or frivolous about this man or his attitude to the world.

TO SUM UP THE
LOOP OF SERIOUS INTENT

If you want to pinpoint the guy who's most likely to succeed, whether as Chief of Police, President of the Bank or even hit man for The Mob, look for a Loop of Serious Intent on a pair of good, strong hands. Their owner won't let you down. No doubt he's dependable, business-like, reliable, dutiful, and gets the job done. He has a sense of responsibility towards all aspects of life, whether it's his position as head of the family, his role as proud father who wants his kids to succeed, or his progress in a career he has chosen carefully.

Whatever he does, he performs to his utmost ability and takes pride in. He's not a slacker and he hates being out of work. If he's an athlete, he's the first one at practice and he's intent on winning for the home team. When there's a deadline, he hunkers down to meet it. If there's a down side to the Loop of Serious Intent, it can occur when combined with a Short Index Finger (see Chapter Ten). But your love and support can help wash away the pain.

BOTH LOOPS: GOOD HUMOR
AND SERIOUS INTENT

People who have both of these skin ridge patterns are lucky indeed. It reflects the ability to do a job well and make a go of any career, while also being able to cut loose and relax when the work's over. In other words, they seem to have the best of both worlds—the serious and the frivolous. They are very much defined as having the traits of both loops. It just happens to be a particularly happy balance for a well-rounded life.

Jerry is a film director who is dedicated to his craft and has gathered a strong group of talented and loyal people for his projects. He somehow manages to crack the whip while also maintaining a great sense of fun that breaks up the tension on his movie sets. His people toil just as hard as he does, for long, strenuous hours. But they always know that Jerry will provide the best food, give them reasonable breaks, and throw one heck of a wrap party when the film's finally done. They'll always come back to work with him again. Jerry has superb examples of both the Loop of Serious Intent and the Loop of Good Humor in his hands. He's a successful director and a popular boss.

THE ANIMAL AFFINITY MARK

There's another skin ridge pattern, most commonly found underneath the Ring Finger. Don't get this confused with the Loop of Serious Intent. It is shaped more like a keyhole. It is referred to as the Animal Affinity Mark *(Queen of Diamonds)*. This doesn't necessarily mean that the owner has a house full of pets, though many who have this marking do love animals of all kinds. This mark is an indication that animals trust this person and feel at ease with them. If someone has this mark in *both* of their hands,

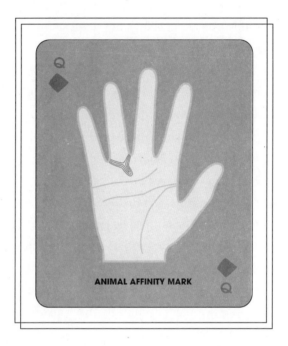

ANIMAL AFFINITY MARK

there is a good chance that they are involved with animals in the workplace, such as a horse trainer, a vet or a dog breeder.

This is a nice marking to have. Anyone who is trusted by animals would seem to be a good bet as a partner or pal. Most of the people I know with the Animal Affinity Mark do have a great love of furry friends and are the first to bend over and pet a passing animal affectionately. It's almost an involuntary gesture as they seem to be tuned into the animal world in a special way.

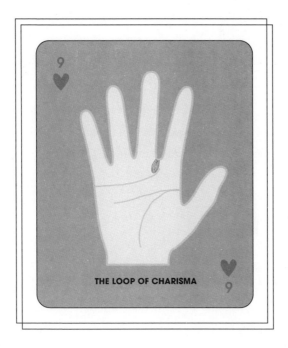

THE LOOP OF CHARISMA

The Loop of Charisma is found between the Index and Middle Fingers *(9 of Hearts)*. It's the most rare of the skin ridge loops. Think of someone you know who commands attention, even if they're not especially good-looking. Somehow there's an aura around them when they enter a room and people are drawn to them.

WHAT IF HE HAS NO SKIN RIDGE PATTERNS IN HIS PALM?

About fifteen percent of people don't have any skin ridge patterns in their palms. It means that they can express a wide range of behaviors, sometimes on the serious side and other times on the light-hearted side. What you won't get is the more predictable behaviors and reactions common when a Loop of Serious Intent or a Loop of Good Humor is present.

A man who has no skin ridge patterns is shaped by other influences, such as how his job is going or what effect his love life has on him, and these can all affect his mood. But you can't pin him down the way you can when a loop is found. For those with these patterns in their hands, from the moment they wake up in the morning, until their head hits the pillow each night, they feel the influence of what their skin ridge patterns denote. Those without any pattern are freer agents, but still prone to the winds of emotional change and influence that life tosses their way.

Again, it's interesting to check his passive hand for the patterns to see if he was under such an influence as a child. Many people have the patterns in only one hand.

HOW DO THESE SKIN RIDGES AFFECT YOUR RELATIONSHIPS?

The traits associated with these skin ridge patterns overlay all of a man's other characteristics. Since a Loop fingerprint guy is already jovial, having a Loop of Good Humor in his palm will make him even more so. And a Loop of Good Humor in the hands of a Whorl guy will take some of the edge off his intensity. Found in the hands of an Arch person, you could be looking at a plumber who moonlights as a stand-up comic, since the Arch makes practical use of whatever skills or talent he has. As you look at more hands, it will become second nature to synthesize all that you see. These skin ridges are especially important to understand if you're dating someone and seriously considering marriage.

Countless studies on marriage have concluded that married people are happier than singletons. It may just be that happy people are more likely to get married than the cranks among us. Or maybe the tendency to find a partner who is very similar to us makes the world seem like a brighter, more wonderful place. We can only guess.

Nobody wants to wake up in the morning with a grouch. When one partner is feeling tense or depressed, angry outbursts can occur. You can't read his mind and the mind is what triggers his emotions. But you can find clues by knowing what's in his hands. There is no doubt that those with the Loop of Good Humor are less likely to wake up in a bad mood, whereas those with the Loop of Serious Intent, especially when it's found with a Short Index Finger, function better overall when things run smoothly.

What if you have a Loop of Good Humor in your hand and your boyfriend has a Loop of Serious Intent? When he sleeps over at your place he sometimes wakes up snapping like a turtle and you're Little Miss Sunshine. It's possible that he may be awakening from nightmares, given his responsible approach to everything. And if he's got Short Index Fingers (see Chapter Ten), then he's a worrywart. These differing patterns are not an impediment to a happy relationship. In fact, you both have something different and positive to give each other. The fact is that you can't keep a sunny person down for long and this is a good influence for your guy in order to balance his sober attitude. As long as you have other compatible features, you can make a success of this partnership if you are loving and tolerant.

In the following chapters, you will learn about other indications in the hand that can either balance his serious nature or exacerbate it. This will help you to make a decision as to whether you can live with him long-term. While it's true that few people want to alter their behavior, a man who loves you should be willing to work on minor problems. Don't try to change a man's basic character. But he can change the way he responds to you so that quarrels are avoided.

It can be delightful for a serious-minded person to be partnered with someone who sees the glass of water half-full. And the fun-loving partner gets to have a real anchor when it's needed. At the same time, a marriage where both the husband and wife share the same skin ridge patterns does seem to keep the glue in their relationship strong.

———·———

THE ROOTS OF HAPPINESS

In his important book, *Emotional Intelligence*, Daniel Goleman gives practical advice on the pursuit of real happiness. He suggests that emotional competence plays a big role in forging a successful life. Long-term studies of hundreds of children brought up in every kind of dysfunctional family show that those who survive best are resilient and tend to share key emotional skills: a sociable nature that attracts friends, self-confidence, an optimistic persistence even when things are going badly, the capacity to rapidly recover from an upset and, finally, an easygoing nature. Goleman insists that these are things that can be taught.

He says that the worrywarts among us will have the hardest row to hoe. In tests of simple tasks, people with confidence tend to barrel along and whistle while they work, whereas those with anxiety keep thinking, "I'll never be able to do this."

So hope is like a buffer against anxiety and defeat and depression. And we can all learn to foster hope, both in our own lives and in the lives of those we love, as we encourage and nurture them and they respond to us in turn. This is something the Loop of Good Humor partner has to offer her Loop of Serious Intent mate. And for some reason, both the Loop of

Charisma and the Animal Affinity Mark seem to give their owners some protection against depression. Maybe it's the extra
attention they get from both people and animals, but having
either of these loops is definitely a plus in the game of life.

If hope and optimism lead to happiness, where do we find the
key to optimism in these stressful and chaotic times? Martin
E.P. Seligman is a Professor of Psychology at the University of
Pennsylvania and a best-selling author. His book, *Authentic
Happiness*, focuses on the importance of optimism and how to
attain it. You won't be surprised to hear that in a study of happiness levels among 225 students, the top ten percent had a very
fulfilling social life. They spent the least amount of time alone
and were rated highest on good relationships by themselves and
by their friends. Ninety-six percent of this group had a current
romantic partner. That's a pretty strong indicator of the potential
for a lasting marriage in their future.

Focus on the gratitude you feel for all that life has given you;
your good health, steady job, loving family, even pets that adore
you. By thinking about how lucky you are to live in a land of
plenty you've got a good start for increasing your sense of well-
being. A simple exercise is to buy any daily newspaper and
compare the things you read about to your own life. It can take
less than two minutes to feel very grateful and happy to be
alive. When you can't stop ruminating over past events and
betrayals, there is no space left for optimism and serenity to
seep up and flood you with happiness. I've mentioned these
important studies on the keys to happiness because optimistic
people attract friends and so have a better chance of getting

married and staying married.

Professor Seligman believes that the late twentieth century attitude that built up self-esteem in children without good reason, that told them to blame others at the drop of a hat rather than taking personal responsibility for their actions, and that encouraged individualism at the expense of, say, altruism or a sense of community, has contributed to unprecedented high rates of depression in the prosperous nations.

When things fall into our laps with no effort required we don't feel any sense of achievement. We just feel empty. This may be the reason why so many people throw in the towel and divorce at the five-year mark. They don't have practice at working hard and watching their efforts pay off. But they've got plenty of practice at pursuing pleasure.

No doubt this is a contributing factor to why young men seem to have lost interest in marrying and having a family. The culture simply does not encourage people to be modest and self-effacing, to sacrifice their personal desires in the name of a higher good. The culture exalts the self and it exalts personal success. For young women today it just may be more difficult to marry successfully than at any other time in history.

In Chapter Nine you will read about the single most important factor in the breakdown of close personal relationships. And you will see that the freedoms of the modern world contribute to the way men feel about women today. Young women can enter the profession of their choice the way young men have always done, can tattoo and pierce their bodies without a murmur from grandma, can yak into their cell on a bus about their intimate lives. It might be a good idea to put yourself in the shoes of a young man these days. There is no longer any taboo connected to a woman expressing her feelings in public, but when it's aimed at her boyfriend the results can be disastrous. No man wants to be belittled, especially in front of others.

The *National Marriage Project* interviewed sixty young men from a variety of backgrounds and ethnic groups. They found that the men had a distant goal of marrying one day, though none had a burning desire for children. Most expressed fear of divorce, and said they thought living together is the way to find out if two people are compatible for a longer-term relationship. For them, living with a girl means regular sex and financial help but they told the interviewer that it also allows them the freedom to look around for someone better.

It seems that society no longer encourages or pressures men to settle down. Today a young man can have casual sex, known as *hooking up*, or he can move in with a girl without the benefit of marriage. Though they say that they'd like to marry one day, these men are in no hurry. They're reading men's magazines filled with the faces and bodies of supermodels and film stars, but they'd like to find a girl who looks good and loves them for who they are. Many of these young men feel they should have a home before they find a wife. But most of all, they feel pretty content with the life they have as a single man today, able to keep their paycheck for their own pleasure and with sex available with no strings attached.

So how are you going to convince one of these men that they should choose to settle down with you? One of the things you

can do is to listen to what men say about what they really want.
The men were of the opinion that girls they met in bars were
only available for sex and weren't marriage material. For a serious mate, they prefer to be introduced to someone through
friends and to get to know her before having sex. Formal dating
has generally been replaced by hanging out with a girl until you
feel comfortable with her, and then asking her for a serious
date.

While almost all the men agreed that it's common for young
people today to have casual sex, they also said that if a woman
sleeps with them on the first date, they lose respect for her
because they feel she's probably doing it with everyone. They
prefer to get to know a girl by waiting for four or five dates
before sleeping with her. Although these men appear to be holding off marriage, most of them expressed a desire to marry one
day when they find their soul mate. They described a soul mate
as a person with whom they feel completely comfortable, who
accepts them as they are, and does not attempt to change them.

The good news is that these men said they were in favor of
education that teaches how to have and sustain a successful
relationship and marriage. It seems that today's young men ulti-
mately want exactly what young men have always wanted, a loving and uncritical partner-for-life. The difference for their generation is that, just as they have a three-hundred channel universe, sixty flavors of ice cream, and unlimited access to information on the Internet – things their own parents never dreamt
of – so too they seem to have an endless opportunity for dating
and casual sex. What male would turn this down? Perhaps the

answer to that is the man who has found a woman who loves and admires him, a woman with whom he feels comfortable and safe, as if he has somehow come home.

Dr. Richard Wiseman conducted tests to find out why some people are lucky in love and find their perfect partner in life while others are unlucky and experience an endless string of unhappy relationships. As part of his ongoing research into the psychology of luck, Dr. Wiseman devised a questionnaire measuring key aspects of people's psychological make-up, such as their levels of extraversion, optimism, intuition, etc. One hundred lucky and unlucky people completed the questionnaire and then imagined that they were about to go on a blind date.

They were shown a fictitious date's questionnaire scores and were asked whether they would like to meet the person. Unlike the unlucky participants, lucky people showed a very strong preference for those who had a similar psychological make-up to themselves. He said that these people were lucky in love because they are instinctively attracted to partners who are psychologically similar to them, and research shows that such similarity makes for a successful relationship. After studying the handprints of long-time married couples I agree with him on this. The next chapter delves into more detail about this phenomenon.

CHAPTER FOUR:

Hand Shape Reflects His Character

When we fall in love, it is most often with a person who is like us. Many people who feel a strong chemical pull towards another person eventually discover they have a lot in common: intelligence, physical attractiveness, values and social skills, as well as odd things like the brand of water they drink or the way they stock their cupboards.

Just take a gander at the wedding announcements in the Sunday *New York Times*. It's amazing how one gap-toothed darling with a widow's peak manages to find and marry his look-alike soul mate. If you gaze at enough photos of newlyweds, it starts to look like they could be related. Check out their smiles, the shape of their eyes, or even the tilt of their chins. There is often a strong sort of "family" resemblance even when they are from different ethnic backgrounds.

And when you consider the intimacies involved when living with another person, it makes sense that we need to share common ground. Helen E. Fisher, in her book, "Why We Love" says that scientists have established that mates who have genetic similarities have fewer miscarriages. They also give birth to more children, and to healthier babies. It's true that we're often drawn to, and get excited by, someone who seems "different" or "exotic," such as a guy from another culture or one who is outgoing when we are shy. But if you date him and get along well, chances are you'll discover that he shares your sense of humor, love of movies, and even political leanings, many traits which can be reflected in your hands.

In fact, this example of the wedding photos is a good analogy for matching your hands to his hands. What you want to look for is not an identical twin, one whose hand features are exactly like yours. You want to find a man whose features are similar enough that you have things in *common* and other features that are *compatible* enough to ensure a long-term commitment. Different, but also similar and compatible—like sweet and sour, or sugar and spice—is an attractive package.

It is also true that we are often drawn to a partner who awakens deep memories of our emotional past, an actuality that can work for us or against us. For example, if your date takes you skiing, and winter sports were the happiest times with your dad, the same can happen. You'll feel instant attraction to any man who rings the familiar bells and you probably won't even realize that it's the memory of your most powerful emotional connections that got you tingling.

This phenomenon explains why we're suddenly smitten, for no apparent reason, by a stranger across the room. His body language, facial expression, voice or physical appearance can set us ablaze. This is fine if we had a wonderful childhood, but it could be the road to disaster if we are setting out to repair with a boyfriend the wounds left by dear old dad or mom. Keep in mind that about half of the happy couples staring out from the *New York Times* weddings page will end up in the divorce courts.

Why is it that nagging is associated with women and rarely with men? What mechanism in the female of the species makes us want to improve our boyfriend or husband? It might be because although we are attracted to men who reflect the good aspects of our parents, we're also drawn like a moth to flame towards those with the foibles of our closest kin.

Keep all this in mind as you explore an important hand feature contributing to his basic personality and behavior; his hand shape. The British artist and author, Fred Gettings, came up with this brilliant system to classify hands. It's one of the easiest things to look for when you're checking out a handsome stranger. There are four hand shapes: Water, Fire, Earth and Air. The four types are quite distinct, although two feature energy, the Fire and the Air hands, and the other two reflect a quieter nature, the Water and the Earth hands. Once you've studied them, you'll wonder how you ever got along with any guy without this knowledge. And you'll be fascinated to see that you're mostly attracted to men whose hand shapes are compatible with your own.

About eighty percent of people have hands that fall neatly into one of these four categories. The rest have a mixed hand type, but this is most often a Fire/Water combination, which I'll describe later. Once you begin to look at hands, it won't take long before you become adept at identifying the shapes.

If you want to classify your own hand shape, just slap your hand down on a piece of paper and outline it with a pen. This will clearly show you the shape. But with a practiced eye, you'll soon be able to identify the four types at a glance. Many world leaders and celebrities can be seen waving to the public on television. Studying their upheld hands is a good way to learn to quickly determine the different hand shapes.

The Water Hand: *Long Fingers and Long Palm*

The world's top models have this hand shape, as do many other women known for their gentleness and femininity. Men with this hand shape are thinkers with a quiet nature.

The Fire Hand: *Short Fingers and Long Palm*

Since this is the hand shape signifying energy, both men and women who have it end up with busy lives and challenging jobs.

The Earth Hand: *Short Fingers and Square Palm*

This hand shape is most often found on country people, on those who are in touch with nature and who can be described as down-to-earth.

The Air Hand: *Long Fingers and Square Palm*

This is the most rare of the hand shapes but you can find it on actors, public speakers, journalists, writers, and all kinds of communicators.

THE WATER HAND
(long fingers and long palm)

All of the world's supermodels have a Water Hand *(4 of Spades)*. Since our hands are shaped partly by hormonal influences, these super-feminine women all share this characteristic. Although the Water Hand shape is more common on women, it is found on many men as well. And when you find him, the

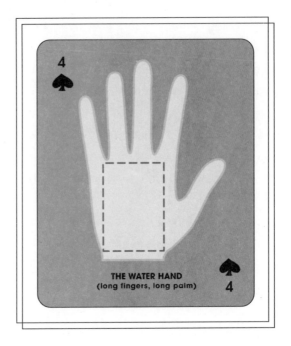

THE WATER HAND
(long fingers, long palm)

chances are good that it will be at a cultural event, in a class-room or bookstore, or that you met him in a chat room on-line. Older books on hand reading refer to the Water Hand male as "the thinker" and looking around classrooms today, it's most likely that the Water hand boys are the nerds.

Being both gentle and clever around a Water Hand man will pique his interest. Having something interesting to say will defi-nitely grab his attention. Men with this hand shape enjoy intel-lectual stimulation. They are emotional, sensitive and respon-sive. Water hand men are commonly employed in professions where they can make use of their knowledge, gleaned both from formal schooling and from a lifetime of reading. They tend to be thoughtful and studious.

Because these men are not aggressive by nature, they make their way through life on their mental abilities and artistic talents. Think of the many gifted painters and writers who produce great art but need a gung-ho agent in order to sell their work. The Water Hand man is not suited to the cut-and-thrust world of sales and commerce. He is the peacekeeper, the mediator, the creator.

If you've fallen for a Water Hand man, he will be gentle, patient and kind. He may even be employed in one of the caring professions, such as the health services or healing. Some become dancers, writers, musicians or poets and many are to be found in IT jobs that require an obsessive attention to detail, for which they are suited. He will be moved by great music, by art and literature and all things beautiful. He probably collects something—rare vinyl, early calculators, or fantasy comics. It's rare to find such a man employed in the competitive business world.

The Water Hand man is more easily hurt in love than men with other hand shapes. Being hypersensitive by nature, he may let his emotions rule his head. Because he is the most romantic of the hand types, he tends to see his lover through rose-colored glasses. He'll be understanding and offer comfort when you need it. Take great care of your gentle Water Hand man. He is the most prone to react to stressful situations. What he longs for is a tranquil home, where he can dream and think and create in peace, with the woman he loves by his side.

Water Hand Lines: Since each hand type tends to have associated line patterns, I'm going to describe these as well. Water Hand palms are most commonly filled with a profusion of fine lines, often long and spindly. Sometimes the palm looks as though a spider web has been laid across it. This large number of lines reflects a busy mind and active nervous system. It is why Water Hand people are so finely tuned to their environment and to other people. It's also why their health is closely tied to the state of their mind and emotions. Remember, this pattern of lines reflects the same general traits as a Water Hand, so if you find them in any other hand shape, you must take this into account when reading the hand.

THE FIRE HAND
(short fingers and long palm)

Remember the agents, mentioned above, who hustle for the gentle artists? You can be sure that these men have a Fire Hand *(5 of Spades)*. They're the go-getters, the bundles of energy who never wind down. There are large numbers of business people, entrepreneurs and politicians who share this hand shape, not to mention firemen, policemen and many performers. Excitement, energy and activity are what these people live for. They find it difficult to stick to routine. If you're checking out men in a bar or at a club, the chances are good that there are a majority of Fire Hand types in this environment. The Water Hand men are at home, curled up with a good book or tapping away at their computer.

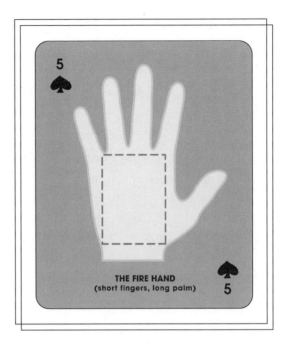

The Fire Hand man is emotional and excitable, has an influence on other people and tends to control situations. He's warm and friendly and draws people to him. He wakes up in the morning and bounds out of bed, ready for anything. He'll take on the world, whatever that entails. This man is both mentally and physically alert and active, and will be for all of his life. When a Fire Hand guy goes to the beach, he won't lie in the sand for very long, waiting to tan. You'll see him sailing, swimming, digging clams or racing his dog into the water.

If you've got your eye on a Fire Hand guy, you're going to have your hands full and can expect a lot of fun and activity. He'll always be up for a challenge and probably likes to participate in sports on a regular basis, even if it's just walking the city. He can be emotionally volatile and throw himself into a love affair at the drop of a hat. But take care, as he can just as quickly lose interest if you can't keep up with his whirlwind pace. He likes to take charge, doesn't like to be told what to do, and tends to do the talking rather than listening. It's not that he has a mean bone in his body, it's just that his natural surge of energy propels him to be an action person.

If you've fallen in love with a Fire Hand guy, lucky you. There aren't going to be many dull moments in this relationship. Keep up with him, both mentally and physically, and he'll adore your company. But be prepared to take care of him when he stretches himself to the max. The Fire Hand man is more prone

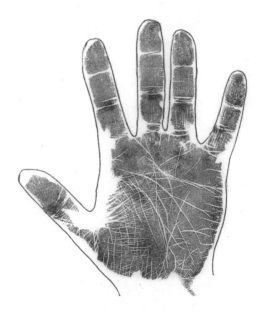

Fig 4.1 *fire hand lines*

to accidents because he's a risk taker and can be impulsive. But at the same time, he is the best suited to cope with stress and can recover from illness and injury better than the other hand types due to his strong constitution.

Fire Hand Lines: (figure 4.1) The Fire Hand palm inevitably contains a large number of strong and clear lines that seem to be cut into the skin. This reflects their dynamism and energy. These lines and line patterns are a reflection of their larger-than-life attitude to everything that comes their way. The depth of the lines is an indication of strength and fortitude, the ability to last when under pressure, and a strong constitution.

THE EARTH HAND
(short fingers and square palm)

Now let's take a breather! Let's pile into the car and take a slow, leisurely drive out to the countryside. Why am I suggesting we go so far away from city life? Because the next hand shape, the Earth Hand *(2 of Spades)*, is most commonly found in rural areas or small towns. These are the men who do nothing in a hurry. Their decisions are formed by a great deal of mulling over the issue at hand. They are attuned to nature and have a strong need to be in touch with the great outdoors. They are stable and predictable and do not like change.

If you've found an Earth Hand man in the city, he'll need a backyard to spend time in, probably gardening or working with tools. He'll be very aware of the weather and the seasons and

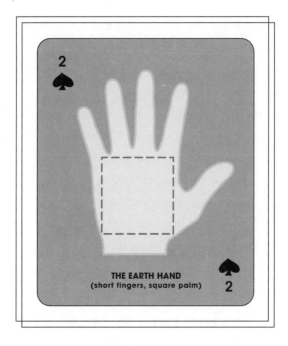

THE EARTH HAND
(short fingers, square palm)

probably talk about retiring to the country one day. There is an almost mystical pull of the land on these people. If you've fallen in love with an Earth Hand man you will need to be his earth woman. Spend hours cooking up his favorite meals and fill the kitchen with the aromas of your labor and he'll never leave you. He'll take his time savoring every morsel and then he'll ask for seconds.

The Earth Hand man gets straight to the point. There's no showing off with those big-syllable words like the Water Hand man. If he's got something on his mind, he'll tell you exactly what it is. Do not think that Earth Hand people are limited in any way because of their tendency to be slow and direct. Their minds can be as sharp as that of any college professor.

Once an Earth Hand person has established a pattern of living, he'll get comfortable in that groove and be resistant to change. So don't expect him to move or to switch jobs at the drop of a hat. It just won't happen. He'll also be skeptical about new innovations or technological changes and tend to stick to the tried-and-true. This is just his nature. He respects tradition. It's what makes him feel safe and secure. For this reason, if there is a need for change, he'll want lots of reassurance, comfort and support from you.

Your Earth Hand man will be steady, reliable and hard working. If he says he's going to do something, it will get done. He enjoys working and gets genuine pleasure out of his labors. He'll be a rock-steady partner in marriage, a good family man. You'll find that he takes a long time to get angry, but when he does, it'll take an equally long time before he cools down. This man has a difficult time dealing with emotional extremes such as a death in the family or divorce. Because of his resistance to change, if things go wrong in his relationship, he won't be the one to walk out the door.

Though Earth Hand people are happiest living in a suburban or country area where they're surrounded by nature, their jobs can sometimes take them into the city. If you end up dating a football or hockey player, the chances are good that he's got an Earth hand. It can also be found on mechanics, miners, construction workers and landscape gardeners.

How do Water Hand and Fire Hand men fit into a small town environment? The Water Hand men will be teachers, doctors or

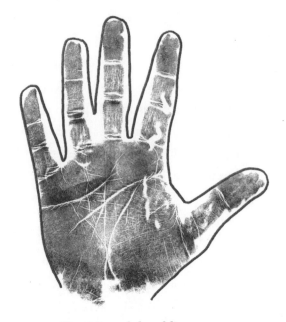

Fig 4.2 *earth hand lines*

librarians. The Fire Hand guys will be in any job requiring energy, enthusiasm and risk-taking, like fireman or cop.

Earth Hand Lines: (figure 4.2) The typical Earth Hand palm contains few lines, cutting quite deeply into the hand. This reflects his stable, down-to-earth nature and a powerful constitution. Country people tend to enjoy good health and probably live longer than their city cousins. This man is generally a doer rather than a thinker or a talker. He's reliable and predictable, just like the coming of the seasons.

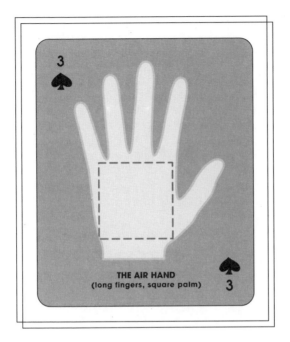

THE AIR HAND
(long fingers and square palm)

We're going to leave the countryside behind and head on back to the city—specifically, any place where the media are found. Communication is of key importance for the man with the Air Hand *(3 of Spades)*. This is his gift, his forte, and his driving force. He is curious, alert and loves to explore and learn. He'll often end up in film or television, in writing careers, public relations, in art, or the travel industry. He may even want to spend his life as an entertainer, whether magician, actor, singer or dancer. If you ever get the chance to enter a television studio, you'll find a great number of Air Hands around you.

If you've got your eye on an Air Hand man, you're going to have your hands full. He's sure to have a low threshold of boredom so you'd better be up on current events and have your own opinions. There's nothing he loves more than to take a topic apart and put it back together again with his own original slant on things. For this reason, he also loves to travel because it adds meat to his knowledge of life. He is fascinated by human behavior and likes to study people and cultures wherever he goes.

Your Air Hand man will have a whole slew of hobbies and always have plans for tomorrow. He'll collect friends around the

Fig 4.3 air hand lines

world and spend a lot of time emailing them to share the latest breakthroughs in the world of ideas. When it comes to love, remember that for this guy an exciting mind is just as attractive as a beautiful face. One night of scintillating conversation can entice the Air Hand man like nothing else.

This is the man who's always asking questions and searching the world for the keys to everything in it. He likes to be involved in different projects simultaneously and can juggle them competently. He's also pretty fearless, but driven more by his raging curiosity than by any innately risk-taking impulse.

Though he appears to have the boundless energy associated with the Fire Hand man, in fact the Air Hand guy more often runs on nervous energy. It is therefore important for him to pay attention to his health. If he doesn't, his body will simply knock him out with something that lays him low until he has recovered his strength and enthusiasm. He'll be prone to headaches and stomach upsets, again due to an overextension of nervous energy. He needs a partner who nourishes his mind and nurtures his soul.

Air Hand Lines: (figure 4.3) An Air Hand is the most difficult to learn to identify. So becoming familiar with its typical line patterns can make identification easier. Most Air Hand palms have many thin lines but they are clear and well-formed. They are a reflection of the curious mind and busy nervous system of the Air Hand person.

THE FIRE/WATER
COMBINATION HAND

The majority of hands that don't fit neatly into one of the four hand shapes above can be classified as Fire/Water Hands (figure 4.4). If you're looking at a person with this hand shape, choose both the Fire Hand card and the Water Hand card for the reading. This is a fascinating individual, with both mental alertness and physical energy. Check carefully to see whether the line patterns in the palm are those of the Water Hand (many and thin as in figure 4.4) or the Fire Hand (fewer and deep as in figure 4.1) and this is the hand shape whose characteristics he will more closely reflect.

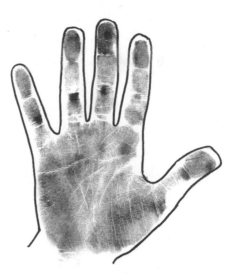

Fig 4.4 *water hand lines with fire-water hand*

Steven has superb Fire/Water Hands. He's a Professor of Mathematics at a University and is gifted at his job. He's always got time for students after class, serves on many academic committees, and is always home on time to take his own kids to ballet or baseball practice. His wife says she wishes she had half his energy. He likes to play racquetball on the weekends or throw a dinner party for many friends.

The deep Fire lines in his palm (figure 4.1), but with longish fingers, are an indication that Steven is basically a Fire Hand person, physically active, with a strong inclination towards mental activity. This is a most interesting and capable hand shape that contributes to a fulfilling and busy life.

THE NUMBER OF
LINES IN HIS HANDS

Once you've focused on a man and decide to investigate him further, he won't mind turning over his palms to let you take a peek. This gives you plenty of time to see the Heart and Head Lines, but what about the rest? If you look at the entire palm you can gauge instantly whether he falls into one of three categories; a hand with *many* lines (figure 4.5), a hand with a *moderate* number of lines (figure 4.6), or a hand with *few* lines (figure 4.7).

I've already explained that the deeper his lines, the more physically vital and strong he will be. The more spindly the lines, the more he functions on nervous energy and relies on

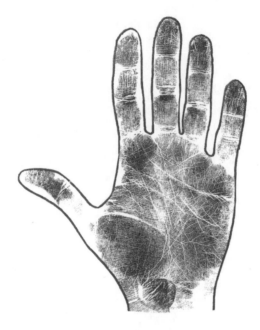

Fig 4.5 *many lines*

brain over brawn. So the other thing you want to gauge is how revved up or how calm he is. If he has hundreds of lines in his palm, he's an active person. He'll be more mentally oriented if the lines are thin and more physically on-the-go if they're deep. If he's got a moderate number of lines, he's neither rapid-fire nor laid-back, but has a nature somewhere in between. And if he's got few lines in his palm, you can be sure that he takes his time, keeps pretty calm and is not a worrier.

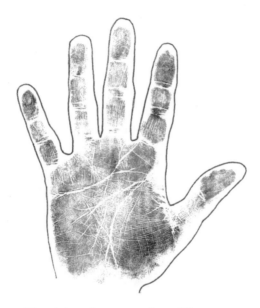

Fig 4.6 *moderate number of lines*

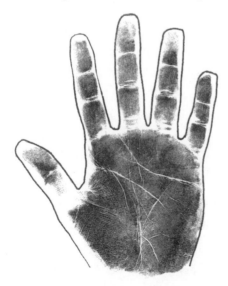

Fig 4.7 *few lines*

FINGERPRINT PATTERNS ASSOCIATED WITH THE HAND SHAPES

As you read this book it will strike you how often a hand has features that reflect related behaviors. For example, you are now familiar with the fingerprint patterns. And I've described the four hand shapes and what characteristics accompany them. Although it's possible for any hand shape to have any of the different fingerprint patterns, it is common to find prints that are compatible with the shape.

A Fire Hand, the one associated with energy, often has prints from the Whorl family. The Whorl is probably the most dynamic of the fingerprint patterns, like the Fire Hand shape. The Water Hand is often found with Loop fingerprints, reflecting an easy-going nature, in synch with the Water Hand need for peace. The very practical Earth Hand commonly sports Arch fingerprints that strengthen his stable, cautious and practical nature. And finally, the Air Hand is likely to have Loop and Whorl family prints, indicative of both sociability and intellectual curiosity.

When you find a hand shape that is not easy to categorize, it helps to be familiar with both the line and the fingerprint patterns most commonly found with the different shapes, in order to pinpoint the shape. Of course, you will come across exceptions, such as the Fire Hand guy with Arches (who may be an electrician who builds canoes in his backyard) or the Water Hand with Whorls (which could be the Art History teacher who has a secret crush on the professor of Classical Literature).

The amount of information you have about a man, with just his fingerprints, skin ridges, hand shape and line patterns, is astonishing. When you compare all of this with your own hands, you have quite an accurate picture of the compatible aspects of your natures as well as how you differ. Let's take a look at the general compatibility of the four hand shapes, while always keeping in mind how your other features mesh.

WHAT ABOUT COMPATIBILITY?

When it comes to hand shapes, like attracts like. Even though there are different combinations that can work out pretty well, and some that seem to do superbly, it's a simple fact that most of us end up with a compatible partner who has a similar level of energy and attitude to life. These are reflected by our hand shapes and line patterns.

AIR AND FIRE HANDS

I've already said that the Air and Fire Hands are the ones that reflect the most physical and mental energy. These people are always on the go, fast and furious, quick and curious. They need stimulation and activity and variety. Only a set of Arch fingerprints will put a slight brake on a Fire Hand guy, but most of his friends won't even notice. He will be doing hands-on sports like kayaking and archery and building a deck in his yard while laying a new patio!

A Fire with Fire or Air with Air hand couple can be very powerful. These people actually stimulate each other and push each other, often into successful working partnerships as well as strong marriages. Yes, sparks can fly, but these people seem to thrive on sparks and stimulation.

As for an Air with Fire combination, it can also work out well. The active mind of the Air partner feeds ideas to the dynamic Fire partner who is ideally suited to carry them out. As long as the Fire partner keeps in mind that an Air Hand needs to rest and recoup at times, to keep his or her nervous system strong, this can be a fascinating and rewarding partnership.

Fire Hand with Water Hand partners can be a challenge. Photos of Princess Diana clearly show her beautiful Water hands while those of her husband, Prince Charles, are Fire hands. When they first met, it was wonderful, that magnetic attraction between two very different types, the energetic Fire Hand man and the gentle, feminine Water Hand woman. Charles would have been under her spell as she cast her eyes demurely downward and hung on his every word. Diana would have looked up and worshipped this fiery polo player who, despite rather ordinary looks, had a physical vitality that was hard to resist. And this energy source would have been aimed squarely in her direction, quite the knockout punch for a sweet and sensitive Water girl. But then they got married.

Diana loved to attend concerts and the theatre, and Charles went along reluctantly. Sitting still in one place for too long can drive Fire Hands crazy. He preferred to be out on the polo field or at the hunt, playing extreme sports with the boys. Diana enjoyed dressing up in spectacularly feminine costumes and spent hours at the beauty parlor or with her New Age therapists. She was a good mother to her boys, but Charles was often away doing his Royal duty. He was a very busy Fire Hand man.

Diana became anorexic and bulimic, worrying about her marriage. The long fingers of a Water Hand orient them to mull things over in great detail, exacerbating any problems and exaggerating them in the process. Diana was the dream goddess for millions of men around the world, but quite unsuited to marriage with a sport-oriented traditionalist like Prince Charles. And he found her quite uninteresting because his idea of a good time was so different from hers.

There was another important factor in their divorce. Diana attracted too much public attention. Charles had never been a crowd favorite simply because he is plain and plainspoken, the opposite of charismatic. But once he began to appear with his new wife, the press almost completely ignored him in their frenzy to photograph the fairy princess. No doubt this development sent his happy hormones into a steep dive, only to be revived in the arms of his mistress.

A Fire with an Earth Hand can make an interesting duo. Although the Fire Hand person is a bundle of energy and activity, the Earth Hand is no slouch in their own way. They are slower-moving, more careful and less boisterous than the Fire, but they inevitably have a quiet strength that can get them through any difficulty.

A Fire Hand male probably has the most adaptable character

of all the four hand shapes. He can survive in a small town as long as he has outlets for his energy, and he can do well in the city in many capacities. This guy can adapt to being married to any of the other hand types, but he's happiest with a partner who can keep pace with his rapid speech patterns as well as his all-night escapades.

The Air with Earth Hand couple is not commonly found simply because of geography. Earth Hand people like country areas, whereas Air Hand people gravitate to the city for jobs in television studios, radio stations, advertising agencies, and publishing houses. In other words, Air Hand people like work that requires communicating. But if an Earth Hand man meets a big-city reporter and the sparks fly, and they have other things in common, they could certainly make a successful union. The Earth influence would stabilize the gadabout Air Hand and she would add spice to his life. If she has Arch Fingerprints, there would be an even stronger bond.

The Air with Water Hand union is both interesting and rewarding. They can establish a deep and abiding love if they make the most of their communication skills and abilities. While it's true that the Water Hand yearns for a slower pace, he will be excited by the happy, busy Air Hand's enthusiasm for life and everything in it. In a long-term relationship, however, it will be the Air Hand partner who will sometimes have to rein in the energy and ideas to accommodate the Water Hand's need for calm.

WATER AND EARTH HANDS

The Water and Earth Hands are found on those who are more reflective, stable and careful. These people take the time to smell the roses, look into a night sky and name all the constellations, or gaze into your eyes and see your true beauty. They're not always on the tear, looking for the next challenge like their Air and Fire buddies. These men are comfortable to settle down with their woman and make a nest. Once they're safe and secure, then they might strike out for wider horizons.

Earth with Earth Hands is, of course, a great pairing. These two will be in synch with both the seasons and with each other. They won't push their partner for regular updates on the state of the world or expect them to enter a triathlon just for fun. They'll savor the delights of home cooking and canning and move at a shared leisurely pace.

Water with Water Hand couples is a wonderful combination, bound together by a common interest in things of beauty, art, and the realms of thought. They'll love to spend lazy Sundays in bed together, sharing the newspapers or watching favorite old films. They'll move at a similar pace, have the same attention to detail, and be sensitive about one another's needs.

Earth with Water Hand partners sounds like a natural combination, but they have the most differences of all the combinations. An Earth Hand finds his strongest affinity with the countryside and nature. For the most part, they are reserved and not big talkers. By contrast, a Water Hand enjoys the stimulation found in cultural pursuits, in books, or being bent over a keyboard, mouse in hand, mentally a million miles away from earth. So it's the mental activity and the preference for country life over city life that brings challenges to this union.

Since they don't gravitate to the same environments, it's not common for these two to meet. But if they do fall in love and manage to take their differences in stride they can make a successful team, such as the football star who marries the beauty queen. If they invite you to a party in their home, you'll find the Water Hand in her spotless and beautifully decorated kitchen cooking up exotic hors' d'oeuvres while her Earth Hand husband takes guests out back for a run on his new John Deere and a few rounds with his Winchester .303.

THE EXCEPTION TO THE HAND SHAPE RULES: WATER HAND WOMEN

The Water Hand female is the most feminine, sweet and gentle of the hand types. She is very much sought after by men of *all hand types* because of her beauty and gentleness. Many of the world's most alluring actresses and models have Water Hands. And if a big husky Earth or Fire Hand guy marries her, she will go off with him to the ends of the earth if she truly loves him, and she can make a success of the marriage. The Water Hand woman is the peacemaker, the superb homemaker, the caregiver. She can marry any of the hand shapes and will always do her best to make it work.

However, since she is also the most easily prone to contracting illness when under stress, it is important that she be aware of how her emotions are affecting her well-being. While the Fire Hand female tackles aggression head-on, and the Earth Hand woman lets it slide off her strong back, the Water Hand woman will do anything to avoid conflict. Because of this, she is the last one to leave a bad marriage, even long after everyone else has advised her to go. The Air Hand woman handles stress uniquely; on the outside, she puts on a confident face, even if inside her nerves are quaking. She's a survivor, maybe thanks to all the knowledge she constantly soaks up. She can hold things together with sheer willpower and positive thinking, but she definitely needs to rest and recoup when her energy is low.

SUMMING UP THE HAND SHAPES

The more hands I read and couples I see, it never ceases to amaze me how Mother Nature so cleverly works things out. The more hands you look at, you will soon discover that many features reflecting the same qualities are often found in one hand. For example, the Fire Hand man can have other indications of an impulsive nature besides his short fingers, such as stumpy thumbs and a space between his Head Line and Life Line. What it all adds up to is that his hands reflect dynamism and energy and impulsiveness.

If you take the time to read the hands of your partner well in advance of any wedding bells, there is every chance that you can learn enough to make a success of the relationship. It will also help you to avoid pitfalls or even to run screaming should it be obvious that you're the mismatch of the century. There are some men who are flexible and adaptable, and others who will never budge an inch in any direction. There are men who can make love on a church green and others who cannot hug a woman in public.

Look at how much vital information you now have from his hand shape and line patterns, as well as his fingerprints, once you have matched them with your own. No matter what his character, there is nothing else in the world that turns a man on like having a woman uphold him, respect him, and love him for who he is! If you think he's a piece of clay that you can mold to your expectations after the marriage, think again. This is not the way to enter into any serious relationship. Learning to read hands will teach you that and also, hopefully, to respect the spirit that resides inside the handsome creature you've chosen to love.

It's not a good idea to nag or whine because a man sees this as a disparagement of his character. I don't think anything scares a man more than when his wife says, "Let's talk!" This holds the threat that things must be going wrong and that somehow he's to blame. Open communication is the best way to keep emotions from spilling over, but there's a way to speak with respect to each other that beats letting it all hang out. Listen to what he says and then ask him to listen to you. It helps if he holds you in his arms while you talk.

Many couples stop kissing and cuddling as the years pass by.

Yet human touch is something that keeps us feeling alive, loved and healthy. Having your boyfriend hold you close, even if you have to ask him, perpetuates a feeling of trust between you. It's all too easy to let petty bickering over everyday hassles put up walls that become barriers to physical intimacy. Once kissing and cuddling get put on hold, sex isn't far behind.

It might be a good idea, once a month, to read through your partner's cards. This way you can concentrate on all of his good qualities and feel happy that he's in your life. It may provide clues as to why you had a falling-out and help you to see him with fresh vision. Looking at your man in a clear and objective light can re-ignite the sparks you felt when you first met him.

CHAPTER FIVE:

Getting to the Heart of the Matter

It would be great if we could read a guy's mind. But being able to read his hands can be just as revealing. In this chapter we're going to deal with a sure indicator of his emotional, romantic and sexual nature, the Heart Line. This line is easy to check out when a man uses his hands to gesture.

Men have two basic needs. They need love and they need work because these are the sources of their personal power. And work often takes priority over love.

Both love and work are linked inextricably to a man's ego over the long-term. While having sex with a gorgeous woman makes him feel good in the short-term, there is no substitute for the rewards of a great career and from having a genuinely caring woman in his life. Only his job will ever give him as much satisfaction, feeling of identity and sense of purpose as finding and keeping his soul mate and raising a family with her.

John Gray, author of *Men Are From Mars, Women Are from Venus*, says that men define themselves through their ability to achieve results. That's why they are always doing things to prove themselves and develop their power and skills. Men experience fulfilment through success and accomplishment. He says that while women fantasize about romance, men fantasize about fast cars, gadgets and powerful technology. Most important of all, Gray states that to feel good about his "self," a man must achieve his goals by himself. Someone else can't achieve them for him.

Gray insists that giving a guy unsolicited advice presumes that he can't figure things out for himself. A man needs to feel

competent at all times. Telling him what to do or how to do it
better makes his sexy and happy hormones (testosterone and
serotonin) plummet. This makes you wonder how any man can
stay happily married to an intelligent, opinionated and outspoken woman. The truth is that some men can handle it more easily than others. When you read Chapter Ten, you will find out
for the first time how you can gauge your man's susceptibility to
criticism.

A man's underlying fear of being seen as weak or being
proved wrong probably explains why men like to talk about
things that are familiar and that they know best. Ever notice
how guys in a group yak about cars, sex and sports? How can
they go wrong? They get to relive their team's win and brag
about hot cars and hotter women. What's the chance of being
shot down by your buddies over this?

Think back to the last talk you had with your man. Many
wives complain that their husband doesn't listen and she has to
tell him things over and over. The fact is that a man sometimes
finds it hard to listen to his wife. He wants to be seen as a hero.
If his wife seems disappointed or unhappy he thinks it's his
fault. When she calls out in frustration that the toaster's still
broken and the kids need new shoes, it confirms his deepest
fear that he is a failure. And his wife has absolutely no clue as
to why he just clammed up. He's trying not to blow a fuse while
still holding onto a shred of his dignity. But she might think that
he's lazy and cheap.

Professor and author Shere Hite produced an avalanche of
first-hand reports on personal, sexual and family issues over the

years. Her 1987 book, *Women and Love,* caused shock waves around the world when women lay bare their true feelings about love and marriage. Almost every single woman said that she wanted more verbal closeness with her lover, to have men talk more about their intimate lives, feelings and plans. Yet as you have just read, all such topics present the possibility that the man will be seen as a loser or found wanting, and that's why he clams right up.

Hite's book states that ninety-one percent of women instigate divorce, although this figure varies according to the research. Karen Karbo in her book *Generation Ex: Tales from the Second Wives Club,* cites a study showing that seventy-five percent of wives initiate divorce. But the fact is, even going back to the recorded history of Puritan times in New England, it is women who leave men more often than men leave their wives.

Almost all the women interviewed, whether married, single, divorced, and of every age, told Hite they have *not yet* found the love they are looking for, that they are hoping their greatest love is to come. So women have a powerful romantic image in their minds of what they want, against which they measure every man. Maybe this unrealistic and romanticized approach to love is part of the reason why women too often dump a man because he's not up to her standards.

Given that all of the above is true, that nothing about men and women living together comes particularly easy once the honeymoon's over, it appears that a woman needs all the insight she can gather. Men don't read self-help books and don't even like to admit that something might be wrong, for reasons that you have just learned. Every man who seriously begins to date a woman probably believes each time that this one is the ideal, that this one will love him unconditionally. There is not a man on the planet that wants to be told he needs fixing.

All men want an available, willing, and adventurous lover. This is pretty well top of the wish list because men are so strongly influenced by their hormones. So how do you get a particular man to focus on you and want only you? It helps to understand his approach to love and sex. His Heart Line can be either Curved or Straight; the first reflects a direct and physical approach to romance, the second reflects a thoughtful or mental approach. Yet every man wants the same; that you show him respect, make him feel important, keep the passion hot, trust him and show that you care exclusively for him. These are basic needs that all men share. It's in the *approach* to finding this special partner that men vary.

THE CURVED HEART LINE

If you've got your eyes on a guy with a Curved Heart Line (*2 of Hearts*), he'll have his eyes on you as well. And his hands before too long! This curving line of emotion is found on the man for whom the physical aspect of love is upper-most in his mind. For this reason, he is also attracted to the best-looking partners. This is the guy who jumps right in there, even if he is on the shy side. He'll find some way to get your phone number or spill his beer in your lap so he's got an excuse to meet you.

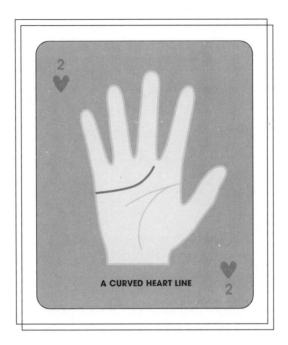

A CURVED HEART LINE

He has an active approach to love and romance.

This man displays his emotions in public more freely than other men. And I mean the whole gamut of emotions. For example, when love is in bloom and you're out together, Mr. Curved Heart Line likes to kiss and cuddle. Once in love, he's more likely to suggest getting married on the spur of the moment on a trip to Vegas than taking the time to plan the perfect wedding.

The physical side of love is very important to this man. If you have a fight, he'll yell and curse in public. Should the relationship end, he'll punch the walls or crash his car and make sure everyone knows he's mad. But in a few weeks he'll be off and running, chasing another beautiful girl and falling in love with renewed passion.

The Curved Heart Line person tends to be the initiator in a romance and likes to get physically involved quickly. He wants affection, love and sex and is quite upfront about going after these with his targeted mate. Throughout the courtship, he takes the initiative by suggesting where they should go and what they might do together. He likes to be the dominant partner and is quick on the draw in every way when it comes to romance.

THE DRAMATICALLY CURVED HEART LINE

The more the Heart Line curves upward, the *more* all of this will apply. If his Heart Line actually curves dramatically upward like a drawn bow, he'll fall in and out of love on a regular basis. In fact, being in love could be the whole focus of his existence. Of course, he's also interested in his beloved as a person, but sex is uppermost in his steamy imagination.

Domenic has just such a Dramatically Curved Heart Line (figure 5.1). He's worked as a teacher for most of his forty-two years. During this time, he has presented himself to the world and to his colleagues as a happily married father of five. The truth is, however, that Domenic has a secret life during the long school holidays. He tells his wife that there is important work to be done in Third World countries where there's a shortage of skilled teachers. And he volunteers his time each summer to pass on his knowledge in places like Thailand, Ecuador and

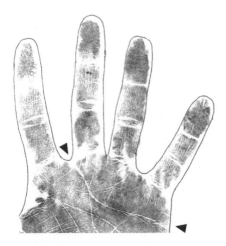

Fig 5.1 *dramatically curved heart line*

Bulgaria. But the truth is, he has been having passionate love affairs with his female students and fellow teachers each year.

These short-lived but highly romantic attachments feed his powerful need to love and be loved with great passion. He keeps a photo album of all his women and shows them proudly to friends outside of his own country. It never occurs to him that he is breaking hearts or taking advantage of these women. He gives each his focused attention and special English classes for as long as they're together.

He brings them gifts and sends them money long after he has left their shores. For the time they're together he loves them completely with convincing devotion. But as the intensity of each affair wanes, he inevitably waves goodbye and returns home, only to live for the tentative excitement of next year's romantic entanglement. He needs to keep the fires of love stoked to a heightened crescendo. When he is at home with his wife and kids, he is a splendid father, albeit one who knows his fantasies will soon be fulfilled again. Not all men with this dramatic heart line carry out their fantasies the way Domenic does. Some throw themselves passionately into a career or hobby so that it takes over their life.

THE STRAIGHT HEART LINE

If you've fallen for a man with a Straight Heart Line *(Ace of Hearts)* you may have to make the first approach. This is the guy who is thoughtful and considerate. He usually takes his

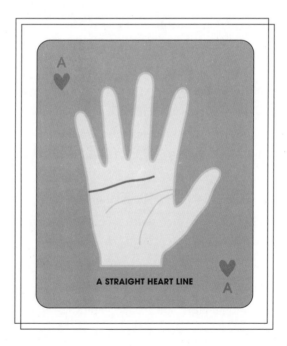

A STRAIGHT HEART LINE

time before asking a girl out. This is because he wants to make sure that you have something in common. He'll ask your friends about you, and if he feels you're interesting, sincere and compatible, he'll want to call you. But if he doesn't, and you feel there's an attraction, don't hesitate to ring him. He'll be happy that you did because it's not that easy for him to make the first move.

Don't expect this guy to be Mr. Take-Charge. He's too considerate for that. He'll ask you where you'd like to go or what kind of food you prefer to eat. This is just the way he's made. Once you have him in your life, he can be just as sexy and passionate as any of those boys with the curving heart lines. But this will mainly occur in private, when it's just the two of you. He'll also be considerate of your preferences, always checking first to see what movie you like or where you want to spend a special holiday.

This man is caring and considerate. He thinks about you and about the relationship and tries to do the right thing to make you happy. He is compassionate, both about you and about the world in general, a caretaker and a good friend. Whereas the man with the Curved Heart Line is passionate in public, the Straight Heart Line lover often prefers to keep his emotions in check till you're alone. Then he can be just as much of a volcano, but his passion will be aimed at making you happy and at loving you with tender care. Once in love, he'll enjoy talking about and planning a very special wedding day to be shared with your family and closest friends and remembered for all of your lives.

The Straight Heart Line guy checks out a woman by listening to her and watching how she acts. He waits until he feels he has gotten to know what sort of person she is before asking her out. And he makes sure the outing is conducive to what he has learned she enjoys. He is looking for compatibility, companionship and sex. He goes about his courtship in a thoughtful manner, always keeping the feelings of his prospective partner uppermost in his mind. The Straight Heart Line man likes to share the power in a relationship, rather than being the dominant person. A Straight Heart Line person may look upon a Curved Heart Line person as a fast mover, even sex-crazy, because he prefers the slow and thoughtful approach to matters of the heart.

More men have a Curved Heart Line and more women have a Straight Heart Line. Simple math tells us that there will be some instances where a Straight Heart Line woman ends up with a Curved Heart Line husband. And there's nothing wrong with that. People do more often end up with a partner who is most like them emotionally, one who has a similar Heart Line. But if we find ourselves attracted to someone with a different form of the Heart Line, understanding what that reflects about their emotional and sexual nature takes us a long way towards dealing with it.

While it's true that some hand readers refer to the Curved Heart Line as being *masculine* because it denotes dominance and the Straight Heart Line as being *feminine* because it denotes passivity, both sexes may have either formation in their hands. It's always amazing to look at the hands of couples in long-time love affairs and see their similar heart lines. It seems that nature draws us towards a partner who is most like us in matters of the heart. At the same time, I have seen very successful and lasting unions between two people with different forms of the Heart Line. So while it is a crucial reflection of your attitude to love, it's not vital to the success of a relationship, as long as the partners are otherwise compatible.

BRANCHES ON THE HEART LINE

If a person has *branches* on his Heart Line it's an indication that his emotional nature is more complicated than most. When

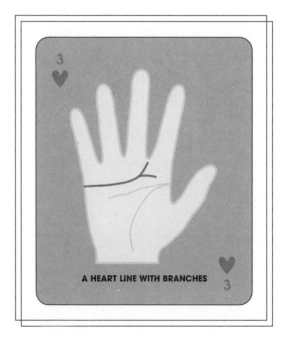

A HEART LINE WITH BRANCHES

there are two branches on the Heart Line *(3 of Hearts)*, it's like having both a Straight Heart Line and a Curved Heart Line. In other words, this man needs to be both physically and mentally attracted to his partner. He has the active, romantic inclinations of the curved line along with the sensitive and introspective qualities of the straight line. He is both passionate and compassionate in nature and in regards to his romantic partner. This is an excellent pattern because it gives an extra depth to any close attachment.

If the Heart Line has three branches (figure 5.2), his emotional and sexual nature will be correspondingly more involved. Simply stated, he'll be like a complex engine that requires more than one intake valve transporting fuel to keep it running smoothly. A man with three or more branches on his Heart Line will look for emotional, sexual and mental compatibility in a

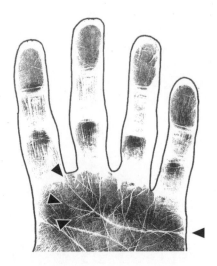

Fig 5.2 *three branches on heart line*

partner. If the search is successful, the chances of establishing a successful marriage are very good. In the meantime, he'll have a good time dating different women who fulfill at least some of his needs.

THE IDEALISTIC HEART LINE

There are a number of people who have the Curved Heart Line ending just to the edge of the Index Finger. It's called the Idealistic Heart Line *(4 of Hearts)*. Being a form of the Curved Heart Line, the owner will have a strong emotional and sexual nature. In addition, he will be particular about who he dates.

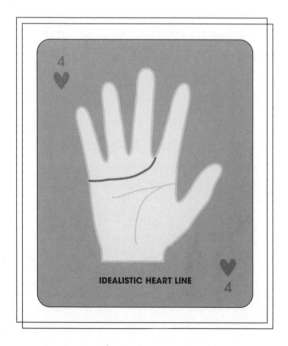

IDEALISTIC HEART LINE

Once he goes out with you, it will soon be evident that you are very special and that he has put you on a pedestal.

This Idealistic Heart Line makes the owner choosy about his friends. Most of us are happy to establish friendships with almost anyone who has common interests, vocation or values. But the Idealistic Heart Line has strong ideas about what kinds of friends are most suited to be part of his life. And he tends to want the very best of everything in life. He has a good idea of what constitutes a perfect romantic partner as well and that's what he searches for. He'll flirt with all the good-looking women at the office but when he finally asks one out, you can bet he has checked out every aspect of her person and deemed her suitable for a successful relationship with him.

The problems arise as the relationship progresses. Nobody is perfect. The first time she turns up for a date in slap-dash attire he may ask her sarcastically if she just got out of bed. So don't get sloppy if you've fallen for this guy. He'll keep you on your toes for sure. He'll look up to you as long as you're his perfect woman and make him proud. If you keep him happy and convince him he's chosen the right one, he will continue to worship the ground you walk on.

A WOMAN WITH
THE IDEALISTIC HEART LINE

If you're a woman with this form of the Heart Line, don't despair if you've reached thirty-five and still aren't married.

Take your time and use your good judgment while on the prowl, because that's the way you are built. Enjoy your years as a singleton and don't worry that you'll end up on the shelf. The fact is that you are single not from a lack of potential partners, but rather because you are finicky by nature. You take a longer time to find your match because you can't settle for less than Prince Charming. And because you do take great care when choosing a partner, the chances of you eventually establishing a strong and long-lived marriage are quite good.

It's best for the woman with the Idealistic Heart Line not to marry young as such marriages tend to occur in haste and without the wisdom that age and experience bring. If you do end up with a man who is not up to your ideal, you will be unhappy and will not remain in the marriage. The other thing to watch out for, once attached, is to take care that you are not overly critical of your partner. Because you've seen and chosen "the perfect man" through your rose-colored glasses, you may find yourself demanding too much from him or being unduly critical. This pressure can make a happy marriage difficult. So pull back the reins if you see this happening. Appreciate and enjoy your fine catch and give him plenty of unconditional love because anyone who is adored will give back in kind.

THE HUMANITARIAN HEART LINE

There's a special form of the Heart Line that stretches across the entire hand. It is called the Humanitarian Heart Line *(5 of*

THE HUMANITARIAN HEART LINE

Hearts) and, in fact, is commonly found on the hands of those whose career is in the service of others. If you've fallen in love with a man with this form of the Heart Line, you must be prepared to share him. This is the man who reaches out to help all of humankind. He is caring and compassionate towards all who need him.

The Humanitarian Heart Line is a sign of selfless idealism. Those who have it care about others and often take up a profession involving such caring. In their romantic affairs, those with this heart line tend to look after their loved ones. They delight in offering care and attention and make devoted spouses and parents. They never get tired from supporting and helping anyone they happen to be fond of, and sometimes fall in love with someone in need of special care.

It is commonly found on healers, social workers and the staff at your local crisis centers or those running shelters for the sick or homeless. You'll find this Heart Line in the hands of missionaries working with the poorest people on the planet. A woman who marries such a man must be understanding of his special heart and the way he gives his time to so many others besides his family.

THE DOWNWARD SWEEPING HEART LINE

Sometimes you can find a Downward Sweeping Heart Line (figure 5.3) that reaches down to touch the Life Line. It's an indica-

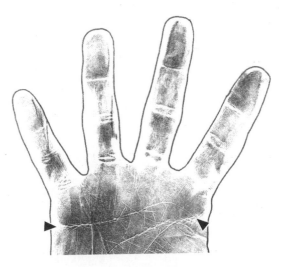

Fig 5.3 *downward sweeping heart line*

tion that the owner can be very easily hurt in love. Some folks can bounce back quickly when a hurt is inflicted on them by a loved one. Not so the person with the Downward Sweeping Heart Line.

It's very likely that he was hurt in the past. Perhaps he was dumped on his wedding day or waited patiently for many years while his love got her degree, only to be cast aside when she took off with another man. It doesn't matter what the traumatic events were, but this Downward Sweeping Heart Line indicates the owner was hurt in the past, and is susceptible to being very hurt by romantic transgressions.

As a result of his particular vulnerability, this man is unusually caring and considerate of other people's feelings. He is the friend who is there when you're in turmoil, the pal who comes to your rescue when your car breaks down. And there is little chance that he will ever do you wrong or break your heart. Having been the victim of emotional angst so many times and felt its pain cutting deep into his soul, he is particularly careful not to bring any such pain into the lives of others.

THE SIMIAN LINE

People who have a Simian Line *(6 of Hearts)* are special indeed, and are both intense and dynamic. This is a single bar line across the palm, that takes the place of the Head Line and the Heart Line. In fact, it is a combination of both lines. The Simian Line is the sign of inner tension, one that can be cre-

THE SIMIAN LINE

ative, destructive or a little bit of both. People with this pattern in their hand(s) often experience difficulty relaxing and commonly report that they have never felt as though they fit in anywhere.

The line can appear as a simple clear bar across the hand or can come in the form of a complex series of lines that, nevertheless, form a bar across the hand (figure 5.4). If you are looking at a hand that does not have a separate line for the Head Line and one for the Heart Line, you can be sure that it's a form of the Simian Line.

People with Simian Lines often display great determination and have a pronounced character. Even though life is not easy

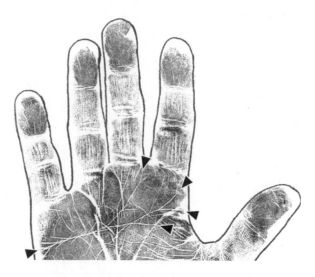

Fig 5.4 *complex simian line*

for them, they can be found among the highest achievers in almost every field. They are known for their passionate approach to life that no doubt contributed to their political or artistic accomplishments.

People with Simian Lines are filled with restless energy. There are no half measures with them. Everything they do is done with purpose and drive. This energy can be released through hard work or dynamic sports like tennis or hockey. A person with this line does everything with gusto, concentrating on the task at hand and plugging away until its completion.

One of the ways to release this energy is through creative endeavors. The owner of a Simian Line feels relaxed when he is focused on creativity. Those who enjoy working with their hands get involved in building houses or furniture. Mentally inclined people with this line write books, music or poetry. Any person with even a trace of artistic talent plus a Simian Line will feel rewarded by painting, drawing or designing. So keep in mind that the Simian Line is an indication of a creative drive. In any group of artists, the chance of finding a Simian Line is higher than in any random group of people.

If you're dating a Simian Line guy, keep in mind that he will have strong opinions. Imagine if every little thing that popped into your head registered immediately in your heart. This is reality for a Simian Line person due to their Head and Heart Lines being one. If he starts to speak about a crooked politician his heart rate will rapidly increase and he may start to shout. For the Simian Line person, it's virtually impossible to stop the emotions from reacting to what is going through his mind.

The Simian line man can be a fine husband and father, if somewhat inflexible. He'll always have the inner feeling of rest-lessness that sets him apart from other people. Remember that creative hobbies are vitally important to him. If he truly loves you, he will rely on you for emotional and moral support because he needs a rock.

Don't try to manipulate him—because you'll learn that he has strong beliefs and sticks to his guns. Understand and tolerate his emotional intensity. Simian Line guys will voice their opinion on any subject, but it's not easy for them to talk about their feelings. You'll have to look to his gestures and deeds to ensure that he truly loves you.

CHAPTER SIX:

More Pieces of His Heart

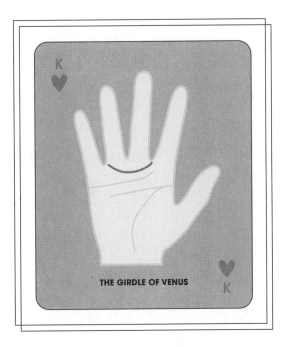

THE GIRDLE OF VENUS

There are other features in the hand that give clues about a man's romantic and sexual nature. Some of these are temporary feelings, but others are a permanent part of his emotional life. It helps to know whether he's hypersensitive, a caveman type or sexually adventurous. The Little Finger is the digit to look for, but remember, there are other things to add into the mix! First, though, don't forget to use common sense when reading hands.

THE GIRDLE OF VENUS

There's a pattern that is sometimes found above the Heart Line, at the base of the fingers, called the Girdle of Venus *(King of*

Hearts). If a man has this formation he will be very sensitive to beauty, art, music and emotional atmospheres. His love life will have many ups and downs due to this sensitivity. He'll react to criticism more easily than most and will be a responsive and tender lover. It's found on poets and actors and highly-strung people. Check out your male friends who have this formation and take notice of their love lives. There is a good chance that these men also have Water Hands and many fine lines in the palm, though The Girdle of Venus can be found in any hand shape.

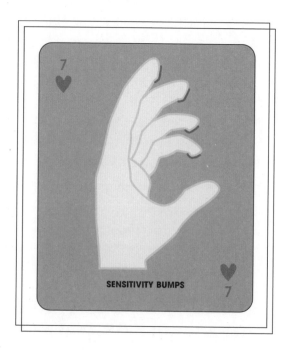

SENSITIVITY BUMPS

SENSITIVITY BUMPS

There are small droplets on the tips of the fingers that are known as Sensitivity Bumps *(7 of Hearts)*. These are found on the hands of artists and poets, dancers and actors, those who are attuned to the arts and beauty in all its forms. People with these bumps respond to music and color with a heightened awareness. They may be prone to skin conditions such as eczema and have a low threshold of pain, because their skin can be hypersensitive to the touch.

THE LITTLE FINGER

Although this is a brief introduction to the Little Finger, it is one of the most important elements in this book. Your Little Finger reveals your capacity to express yourself through writing, acting, and speaking. It is the finger of communication and can be an indication of your suitability for work in sales, business, commerce, teaching, languages, the law, and the media. It is also the finger that reflects your sexuality and how comfortable you are in a relationship or how distressed.

The longer the Little Finger, the more adept a man is at getting his point across, at expressing himself and his ideas. The author Stephen King has one of the longest Little Fingers I have ever seen and he has outwritten even the notoriously prolific author, Charles Dickens. It reaches skyward, almost to the top of his Ring Finger. But for most of us, this digit rises just to the top joint of our Ring Finger. Anything beyond this is considered a Long Little Finger.

THE LOW-SET LITTLE FINGER

Before we describe the Long Little Finger, be aware that some people have their Little Finger set low down in their hand. Normally, you can draw a straight line along the base of the fingers where they end until you get to the Little Finger. In most hands, this finger is set just a bit lower than the other fingers (figure 6.1). But in an increasing number of hands these days, this finger is set quite low in the hand (figure 6.2).

Which reveals an important psychological trait. When the young men and women with this formation grow up, they tend to be attracted to a partner who makes them feel emotionally the

Fig 6.1 *low set little finger*

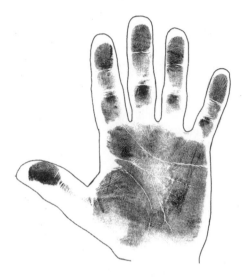

Fig 6.2 *regular position for little finger*

way that their problem parent made them feel. In other words, if
their father demeaned them and told them they were useless
and would never amount to anything, they tend to be attracted
to partners who make them feel inadequate and sad or unsure of
themselves. Once a man, or a woman, understands this mechanism, and the fact that it is tied very deeply to conditions that
were outside of their control as a child, they can make an effort
to over-ride this emotional compulsion.

Psychologists say that people are drawn to a partner who
resembles their parents. So when a man who suffered emotional
problems as a child falls in love, he is trying to work out those
unresolved problems. You can estimate how well a man survived his childhood by looking at his Little Finger. There are
some children who are blessed with a strongly optimistic nature

and manage to come out unscathed. These individuals will have a Little Finger only slightly low-set. But for many men who did not receive the emotional nurturing they needed when young, you will find the Low-Set Little Finger formation. Once again, the lower it is, the more he will feel the need to find a partner who reflects his problem parent's emotional abuse.

It's important to be aware of the Low-Set Little Finger in order to properly gauge the correct length of a man's Little Finger. If it appears to be Low-Set, then mentally raise the tip an appropriate amount. Since the Little Finger is the most important digit after the Index Finger, it is worth making sure you have an accurate assessment of its correct length.

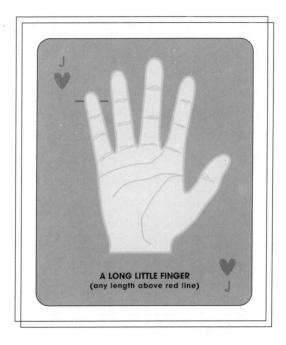

A LONG LITTLE FINGER
(any length above red line)

LONG LITTLE FINGER

If you're dating a guy who is persuasive and charming, with the gift of the gab, check out the length of his Little Finger *(Jack of Hearts)*. Long Little Fingers are usually quite strong and well-formed. If you know a professional writer, take a look at his Little Fingers and you are sure to see a prize pair. A Long Little Finger is also an indication of a strong sexual nature. No wonder a silver-tongued devil doesn't need to be handsome.

Every finger is divided into three sections. It is the upper section that reflects our way with words. When you see an upper third joint of a Little Finger that is longer than the joints below, it will be found on an articulate guy with the gift of persuasion. Successful lawyers, teachers, and entrepreneurs often have this long top joint in their Little Fingers.

LITTLE FINGER STICKING OUT

When you see a hand with a Little Finger Sticking Out *(10 of Hearts)* you can be sure that the owner is under some kind of emotional stress. It is a signal that the heart is unsure, even though the reasons can be many and varied. If the finger is jutting out like a flag, this is most likely a person going through a difficult divorce.

If your little finger sticks out from the rest of the hand it could be the result of problems with your boyfriend; he may be

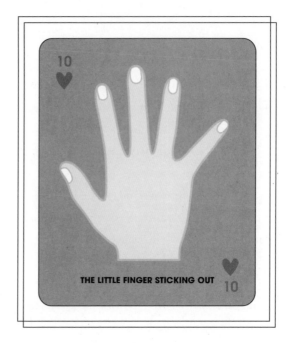

THE LITTLE FINGER STICKING OUT

spending more time in chat rooms than with you, so that you suspect a cyber-affair. Or you may have had a blowout over his parents visit and you think he loves them more than you. Whatever the cause, when you find a Little Finger Sticking Out on any hand it indicates emotional insecurity.

In the case of movie stars, this formation may be due to the constant focus on their sexuality. Take a look at the little fingers of the actors in the next film you watch. Then look at the little fingers of people in the street. It is astounding how many movie stars seem to be in a perpetual state of emotional or sexual distress, though there are exceptions. Tom Hanks and Pierce Brosnan must be lucky in love. Their Little Fingers stand right

beside their Ring Fingers, which reflects emotional contentment.

You will now be able to tell, from a glance at any photo, the
Hollywood couples that are happy and those in the midst of a
falling-out or even a complete meltdown. Halle Berry's Little
Fingers were sticking out the night she won her Academy
Award. It was apparent that her marriage was in trouble. Yet she
didn't file for divorce for another year. The fingers can reflect
what the mind has not yet admitted to because our emotions
come from the unconscious part of the brain. Look back in old
magazines and see Nicole Kidman's Little Fingers sticking out
further and further each year, until they are like flags during the
divorce from Tom Cruise.

The further out the finger is jutting, the more emotional trauma is being felt. When the romantic problem is resolved, this
finger will return to its regular position beside the Ring Finger,
until the next time the love life goes into crisis mode. Then out
goes the Little Finger until its owner feels emotionally secure
again.

This piece of information might seem innocuous but think
about its implications. From now on, you only have to glance
down at your own hand to see if you are truly emotionally
secure in your life and in your relationship. If you keep an eye
on your Little Finger, you will see that its position can vary from
week to week. And if you think back over what has gone down
between you and your lover, you will realize just how accurately
this finger gauges your emotional and sexual feelings.

All you have to do is to shake your hand and then hold it up so that it feels comfortable. If your Little Finger is Sticking Out and you try to rein it in, you will notice that it becomes shaky, until you allow it to wander back to the outward position. Yes, it's true. You can't fool Mother Nature. She has provided this finger as a handy indicator of your inner happiness and contentment, but you never knew it before. Now you do.

You can also check the position of your lover's Little Finger. We can all claim to be happy when we are not. But hands do not lie. So from now on you have a gauge of how secure both you and your partner feel. And when you see a Little Finger Sticking Out you will know it's time to heal a wound. Your lover will be quietly astounded that you are aware of his feelings.

Fig 6.3 *the gapped little finger*

THE GAPPED LITTLE FINGER

Sometimes you'll find a hand where the fingers are held close together except for the Little Finger, which has a gap *(figure 6.3)*. You can see that it's not the same as a Little Finger Sticking Out, because the finger stands straight upward. It takes a considerable amount of time for a little finger to develop this spacing. Both Madonna and K.D. Lang have such a gap. It indicates that they have an unconventional approach to sex and their own sexuality. The gap can also reflect a long-standing degree of discomfort with the emotional and sexual life, such as the angst of a closeted gay man, the pain of a man whose wife hasn't slept with him for five years, or even a teenage girl whose parents openly favor her older sister, leaving her feeling bereft.

SOME OTHER NICE FEATURES

THE SAMARITAN LINES

If you look at the area of his palm just under the Little Finger, you might find a number of clear lines in the skin. These are known as Samaritan Lines *(4 of Diamonds)*. There should be at least four lines and no more than seven and they should appear in a patch or grouping.

Some books on hand analysis use the term Medical Stigmata when these lines are found due to the large number that are

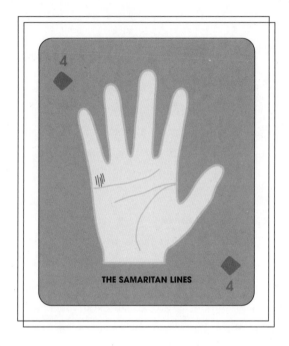

THE SAMARITAN LINES

found among hospital staff. People who have the Samaritan Lines are drawn to the healing professions and are the friends you call on when in need of advice or help. These folks may also be found working in shelters for the homeless or with victims of domestic violence.

Many doctors choose their profession because of the financial rewards and status associated with a medical career. Therefore, it's more common to find these lines on the hands of nurses than on doctors. The lines are also found on naturopaths, chiropractors and others in the holistic healing and counseling professions. But if you do find them on a doctor, you can be sure that

he is a caring and compassionate person who felt a calling to
heal the sick.

Like all the features reflected in the hands, the Samaritan
Lines should be interpreted in the context of his entire hand.
On their own, they denote an inner need to play the Good
Samaritan and may reflect genuine healing ability. This over-
laps with everything else you are learning about him. For example, the Samaritan Lines on a Fire Hand guy could mean he's
racing around for Meals on Wheels in his spare time. The Water
Hand man with these lines may prefer the gentler option of
working the phone lines for a Crisis Center. An Earth Hand
with Samaritan Lines will be the farmer who gives away his sur-
plus crops and lends his tractor at the drop of a hat. And the
Air Hand person with them will undoubtedly write or speak on
behalf of the oppressed.

THE ANGLES OF RHYTHM AND TIMING

If you take a look at any famous musician when he holds up his
hand, you will behold a wonderful example of the Angles of
Rhythm and Timing *(8 of Diamonds)*. The Angle of Timing is
often found on the hands of writers, actors and comedians. Jim
Carrey has angles so pronounced that his hands appear to be
warped.

The Angle of Rhythm reflects a natural sense of rhythm.

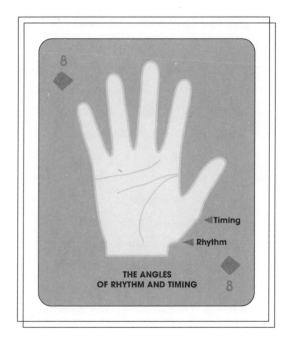

Dancers, gymnasts and born musicians often have *both* of these joints well developed. Take a look at photos of Elvis, Mikhail Baryshnikov, Ella Fitzgerald, Quincy Jones and Eminem or any other great musician or dancer, and you will see fine examples of these angles.

THE SUN LINE

The Sun Line *(Ace of Clubs)* often begins to grow in the hand after the age of thirty, but can be found in the hands of children.

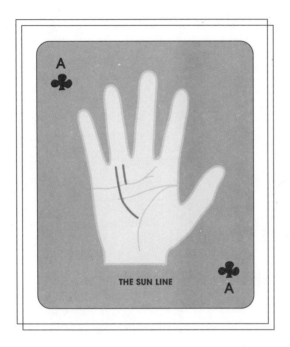

THE SUN LINE

It's one of the lines that can come and go in the hand, but most
often grows slowly over time. This line was traditionally associated with being artistic. Some claim it is a sign of wealth and
fame. The truth is that it can be found in the hands of a movie
star and it can just as easily be found in the hands of a content-
ed poor man.

If there are other indications of artistic ability in the hand,
having a Sun Line will compound them. But overall, looking
back over the thousands of hands I have analyzed over the
years, I have come to my own conclusions about this wonderful
line. It appears that it grows in the hands of those who make a

great effort in life. Whether they succeed financially does not matter. It's their inner or spiritual contentment that seems to make the Sun Line grow stronger.

So this line is an indication that this person never grows bored with life. Rather, the years after retirement will be just as filled with activity and pleasure as the years before. There may also be financial or other success attached to the later years, simply because this person makes an effort to get the most out of life. If you find other indications of perseverance and willpower, there's an even greater chance that the retirement years could be the best of their life.

CHAPTER SEVEN:
Why He Thinks and Acts the Way He Does

Most of us act differently depending on who we are with and how comfortable we feel with them. There are many factors at work that influence behavior. If you were born shy, you're reserved when meeting strangers. Once you get to know them, you'll feel free to express yourself and speak your opinions. So the degree of timidity is an important part of your persona. Most shy people learn to put on a mask when out in public. They fashion it from whatever talent or ability they possess. Even the shyest people can gain self-esteem through their efforts and achievements, yet they always retain the undercurrent of sensitivity when in unfamiliar situations.

We are born with certain characteristics and then embellish these to create our unique personality. Character is reflected in the hands by such patterns as the Loop of Good Humor, the Simian Line and many other features. Being able to read hands gives you a jump-start on what makes a man tick. We all have a degree of willpower and can control or alter our natural impulses, if we choose. Such efforts are rarely sustained long-term, however, as we fall back into the habits that feel most natural. This book gives you a solid introduction to character as it is reflected in the hands. Since character is the person we are when we're at home, and personality is the way we appear to others, it's important to gauge a man's character if you're thinking of living with him.

Our family and peer group influence how we live our lives and the decisions we make in that life. You are about to find out how to identify those men who are not so easily influenced by others. It's a key piece of information because any man who did not listen to his parents or pals is not likely to listen to his partner. Like most aspects of character, there are benefits and drawbacks to being independent, impulsive or a rebel.

Birth order can be an interesting amalgam to hand reading when evaluating a man. Dr. Kevin Leman, in *The Birth Order Book*, puts it all in a nutshell. First-borns share most of the traits of an only child. They are generally perfectionists, reliable, well-organized, critical, serious, loyal, conscientious, goal-oriented and self-reliant. They were once the center of their parents' world and they'll strive for most of their lives to retain or regain this position. A large proportion of first-borns end up in high achievement professions such as architecture or law. It would take several pages to list some of the famous performers, politicians, generals and tyrants who were first-born or only children. They also make up the majority of clients seeking help from counselors.

Many great, gifted, successful or notorious men were either first-born sons or only sons: Beethoven, Shakespeare, Freud, Mao Tse-Tung, Hitler, Nietzsche, James Dean, John Lennon, Goethe, Bob Marley, Ted Bundy, Martin Luther King, Einstein, Galileo, Charles Dickens, Wayne Gretzky and twenty-one of the first twenty-three American astronauts to go into space. The list is endless.

Dr. Leman illustrates the power given a first-born son and his desperate need to retain it. Abbie Hoffman, one of the Chicago Seven and founder of the Yippie Party in American politics, was

a first-born son. For the first three years of his life, the light
from his parents and doting relatives shone only on him. One
day his mother disappeared into the hospital. Shortly after giving birth to her second child, she received a phone call from
home saying that Abbie was "sick" and needed her! So frantic
was her haste to return and attend to the little tyrant's needs
that she forgot to register the birth of her second son, Jack.

Second-borns are generally mediators, independent, loyal to
the peer group, likely to avoid conflict and often end up as
rebels who go their own way. They've survived the jealousy of a
displaced older sibling. While they're sometimes bullied by the
first-born, they tend to hone their survival skills through this
trial by fire. Take a look at any two siblings, a first-born and his
second-in-command, and you're sure to find two very different
personalities. It's almost as though the second-born checks out
the talents of his older sibling and aims for a different way to
shine.

The youngest child is generally charming, a show-off, manipulative and precocious, the family clown, with a tendency to
blame others if things go wrong. Mom and dad were tired by the
time this apple fell off the tree and they tended to spoil him and
let his bad behavior slide. Besides, what a cute little dickens he
was, with those chubby cheeks and adorable big browns.
Everyone just couldn't help but fall all over him when he tod-
dled into a room. As one dad told me when his wife gave birth
to their third child, "I just can't get her out of my arms. She's
our last baby and I want to savor every moment. I grab her
when I'm home from work and she usually ends up in bed with

me and my wife." Discipline flies out the window with the last-born.

If you think about the life patterns attributable to birth order it becomes evident why first-borns so often grow up to be serious achievers, second-borns have a lot of friends and are great negotiators and go-betweens, and last-borns tend to take things easy, go into less stressful careers and sometimes just sit back and wait for the inheritance to roll in. It's perhaps more important today to be aware of birth order when so many families are having only one or two kids, which means an explosion in first and last-born behaviors.

Birth order can be synthesized along with his other characteristics. We're going to take a look at his fingers, whether they're smooth or knotty, long or short, gapped or close together. This provides a wealth of information as to why he thinks and acts the way he does. Like birth order, they're another piece of the puzzle that makes up his character and contributes to his personality. And it's easy as pie to glance over at his hands and check these out. The more ammunition you have about what drives your man, the better able you will be to deal with misunderstandings or emotional problems that crop up.

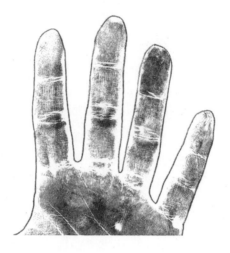

Fig 7.1 *small space between fingers*

FINGER SPACING

You can learn about a man by the way he holds his fingers, either *close* together or *splayed* outward. Most men, when they hold up their hand, will show slight chinks of light between their fingers (figure 7.1). This denotes a normal amount of independence. This guy will take risks when necessary and he'll have a reasonable ability to think for himself.

If a man holds his fingers tightly together so that not even a card can be slipped between them *(10 of Clubs)* he will be careful and not want to change his life unless pushed. He's the guy who takes his time to marry, and once he does, he'll stay longer than other men if things go wrong. He's reluctant to strike out on his own and feels safer staying put. He can get stuck in ruts,

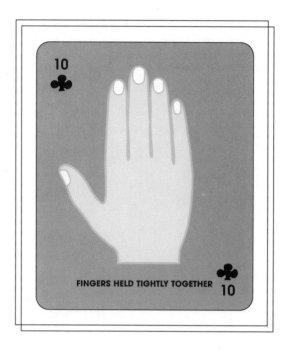

though he won't necessarily complain. It's his security blanket, something he needs in order to feel okay. Despite all this, he can do quite well in life, especially if he gets into a secure job where he can work his way slowly upward. There is something to be said for the approach of the tortoise over the hare.

By contrast, there's the guy who holds up his hand with his fingers splayed outward *(Jack of Clubs)*. This extrovert is the life of every party, jumps at any opportunity that comes his way and embraces strangers like he's known them all his life. He's got the infectious enthusiasm of a young child but can wear others down with his gung-ho personality. Rock star Steve Tyler has this formation, as well as comedian Robin Williams. If you

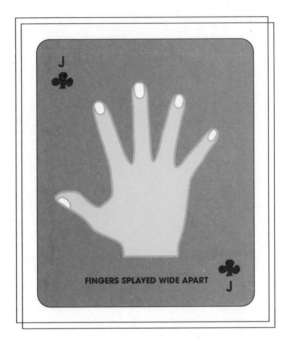

FINGERS SPLAYED WIDE APART

watch a comedian playing a character and that character is a raving extrovert, the comedian will instinctively splay out his fingers to accompany the staccato dialogue. Most small children, before they go to school and develop inhibitions, hold their hands like this. We are all born with the natural joy of feeling alive, but life can knock it out of us.

FINGER GAPS

When you first look at the way people hold their fingers, it might take a while to see the difference between *spaces* and *gaps*. Anyone can hold up his hand and create space by splaying out his fingers. But a gap is when the fingers are held straight up and there are visible openings at the bottom *(8 of Hearts)*.

When there are gaps between all the fingers, you have a non-conformist, someone who picks up a rulebook and tosses it out the window. This man thinks for himself and is not swayed by public opinion or what his friends tell him. Whatever the beliefs or values of the family he grew up in, he found his own path. He was born with an independent turn of mind and nobody can influence him unless he decides he wants to be influenced. Small gaps indicate a good ability to think for your self. The wider the gaps, the more inclined the owner is to ignore social

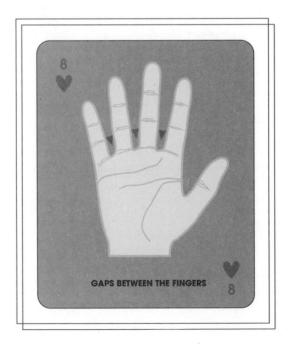

GAPS BETWEEN THE FINGERS

conventions. Musician Eminem has wide gaps between all of his fingers.

Dennis Rodman also has gaps. His career as a star basketball player in the NBA began under unusual circumstances, attracted frenzied media attention, and ended with a bang. Through it all, Dennis has always marched to his own drummer. Nothing he ever did in his life was done according to the rules. By being outrageous, Dennis attracted attention as the star of a game that had been known for its gentleman players. His disdain for the restrictions of conformity led to his dismissal from football, a sport he excelled in and loved to play.

When you find a pattern in the hand that suggests a dramatic character trait such as non-conformity, it must be balanced against the rest of the hand. So you look to see if there are other indications of an independent individualist: Whorl family fingerprints, unusual finger lengths, a space between the Head Line and Life Line or a unique Head Line formation.

If you find one or more of these, then the non-conformity and individuality of the person is exaggerated. Such a guy could be living in a trailer park and singing Rap music based on his life. But if a man with gapped fingers has patterns such as Loop fingerprints and a tied Head Line and Life Line, he could be a suburban husband who buys a Harley and heads to Sturgis every year. In other words, the non-conformity would be expressed in a less dramatic manner. But it would certainly be there.

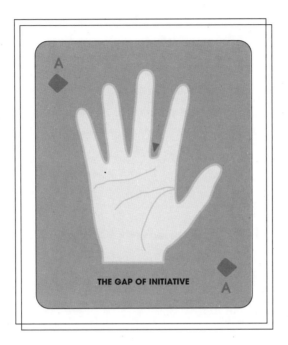

THE GAP OF INITIATIVE

When there is one Gap between the Index Finger and Middle Finger *(Ace of Diamonds)*, you find a very specific ability. This is sometimes referred to as The Manager's Gap and is found on those who can make decisions for themselves and for people around them. Don't get it confused with the Long Index Finger (Chapter Ten) that reflects a born leader. This gap is not found on the big boss. It reflects the gift of initiative. You'll notice that the person with this gap naturally makes decisions and others know this and respect him for it.

If this Gapped Finger is also Short (Chapter Ten) it's an indication that this person was born shy but has made a tremendous effort to overcome this condition. A man who has this formation loves to be the center of attention and needs lots of praise. He may share the managerial skills of the guy with an Average Index Finger, but he won't want any criticism of his instructions or his manner.

SMOOTH OR KNOTTY FINGERS

When you look at a man's hands you can gauge two things very quickly: the relative length of his fingers and whether they are

SMOOTH FINGERS

smooth or *knotty*. This determines how he thinks and the approach he takes to every single thing that passes through his head. So this is a quick way to get inside the working of his mind.

Smooth Fingers *(2 of Diamonds)* are those that do not have knots. These are found on people who use their intuition more than their reasoning powers. Poets, artists, actors, writers and good sales people commonly have smooth fingers. These folks tend to rely on their hunches and their intuition. They have learned that this is a reliable way for them to solve problems or get answers.

People with smooth fingers are creatures of emotion rather than creatures of reason. They tend to rely on their instinct, but can be seduced by appearances. Men with smooth fingers are generally good-natured. They appear easygoing because they don't have a need to analyze every little thing.

Knotty Fingers *(3 of Diamonds)* are ones with pronounced joints (not caused by arthritis). They are at their most extreme if the joints at the top and middle are both developed. They are more commonly developed at the middle joints. They're found on people with a strongly analytical mind. Their owners love to go into great detail and gravitate to careers in science and engineering. Philosophers have knotty fingers. People with these fingers ask such questions as, "How does it work?" "What is it for?" "What does it mean?" and "Is it true?"

Because of their questioning nature they're often labeled as being argumentative, cantankerous, or skeptical. They would disagree and claim that they are only analyzing every situation

in detail, or breaking it down into its parts. This is true. But it does seem like argument to the smooth-fingered folks who rely on intuition. These two finger formations represent diametrically opposed thought processes.

People with knotty fingers think everything through and always have a good reason for their actions. No matter what they say or do, if you ask them why, they will enthusiastically tell you in detail. A smooth fingered person who laments, "No matter what I say you always have a comeback," is referring to his knotty-fingered friend. You don't even have to wind them up. Their ability to go on at length is exacerbated if they have a Long Head Line and/or a Long Little Finger.

If you tell your knotty-fingered pal all of this, he'll feel hurt. After all, this is the way his mind works all the time, even when you're not around. He actually carries on debates when he's alone. It's the way he looks at life, testing, investigating and discussing all aspects of it. He loves to do crosswords, puzzles, and play chess.

Because their minds are so busy, people with knotty fingers can appear to be more intelligent than those with smooth fingers. They probably retain more knowledge because they are always investigating things. The knottier the fingers, the more all of this applies. Some people have slight knots on otherwise smooth fingers, so such a person would be predominantly intuitive but with some analytical qualities. By comparing a few dozen hands, you'll soon be able to differentiate between smooth and knotty fingers.

SHORT FINGERNAILS

Short Fingernails *(Queen of Clubs)* are those that are wider than they are high. They reflect a well-developed critical faculty. This is excellent for many careers where having a sharp and well-honed analytical mind produces results. Newspaper and magazine editors with these nails do superb work. The job of critic, in whatever forum, benefits from this type of fingernail formation. However, in the personal sphere, it's not so warm and fuzzy. A guy with short fingernails will let you know if your dress or hair is not up to par. He will take you to a movie and

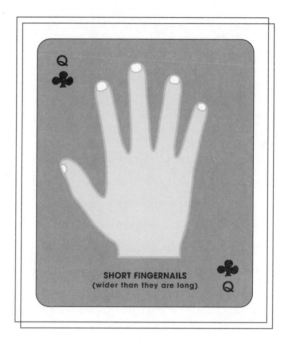

SHORT FINGERNAILS
(wider than they are long)

then tear it to shreds if it falls short of *Citizen Kane*. At the restaurant, he'll rag on the chef if his burger isn't rare. It's amazing how even a mild-mannered, whorl-dominant, bookworm type of a guy, if he has short fingernails, will still hand out quiet appraisals of everything in his path.

Like with knotty fingers, this formation of the nails inclines the owner to an analytical mind. You can't change this part of his nature. These people are rarely dull because they've always got an opinion. If he's got both the knotty fingers and the short fingernails, beware if you are gentle, sensitive and high-strung. This man is best partnered with a like-minded woman who also lives to debate and critique.

FINGER LENGTH

Once you begin to study hands, particularly when you know the four hand types, you'll be able to judge finger length. At first, you'll probably find yourself exclaiming, "Wow! She's got stumpy fingers!" or "Gee! Look at those long digits!" You will be surprised by the endless variety of hand types, finger and palm lengths, that you had never noticed before.

The length of a person's fingers is relative to the whole hand. A Fire Hand has fingers that are short when seen in contrast to its long palm. A Water Hand has fingers that are as long as, or even longer than, the long palm. So when you look at a hand and concentrate on the finger length, you see it in relation to the shape of the palm.

Fire Hands with short fingers tend to be impulsive and like to do things quickly. They think fast and can quickly grab the essence of whatever is being discussed. Short-fingered people look at life on a big scale and can oversee large projects because of the bird's eye view they take of the world. They are action-oriented. The Earth Hand with short fingers does all of this on a much slower scale, probably in tune with the seasonal changes.

Those with long fingers take their time and mull things over. They focus in on a project and go to great lengths to check out every aspect of it. They're detail-oriented, patient and thorough when performing a task and will work diligently until it's done. Some of them are obsessive-compulsive.

THE HEAD LINE

As you've learned, lines in the palm are not as important as the fingerprints, skin ridges, and hand shape when determining character traits. One exception is the Heart Line, which does give vital insight into a man's emotional make-up. Another exception is the Head Line, which can also give you helpful information about the way he thinks.

There are as many Head Lines as there are people on the Earth. But in order to determine what kind of thinking patterns a man has, we're going to reduce this to the length of the line, the direction and the flexibility.

A Long Head Line *(4 of Clubs)* is a sure sign that this guy thinks in a detailed and careful manner. Short and snappy is not his style. He can talk about a wide range of topics and interests. When the Head Line is really long and teamed with knotty fingers or a Long Little Finger, then you may as well just sit back and enjoy the show. If he's bright and well-informed, it will be a delight. If he's not, you may want to run screaming. But he will be inclined to lecture, perform, recite, inform and pontificate.

A Short Head Line *(5 of Clubs)* reflects a simple, practical, and straightforward manner of thinking. It is called The Engineer's Head Line if it ends very abruptly. Men with this formation are certainly brilliant at cutting to the chase in the field of design. Ask any woman who is married to an engineer and she will confess that he's no Shakespeare. He addresses the issue at hand with a no-frills approach and deals with essentials. This is the Head Line of the problem solver.

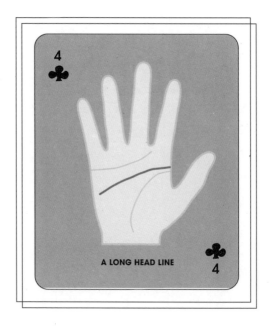

A LONG HEAD LINE

A Straight Head Line *(2 of Clubs)* is the sure indication of a clear and concentrated manner of thought. The man with this pattern gets right to the point, regardless of whether the line is straight across the hand or sloping downward. He will be stable and practical. In the business world, this type of Head Line was once quite common. When it goes straight across the palm, the owner focuses on the material world and fiscal success. He applies the same hard-headed approach to finding a suitable woman.

A Curved Head Line *(3 of Clubs)* is found on men who like to explore new ideas and concepts and have a flexible approach to everything. In the modern work world of high-tech innovation,

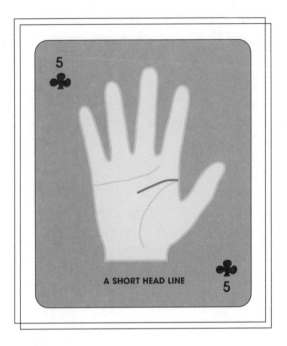

A SHORT HEAD LINE

this head line reflects the ability to combine imaginative fantasy with common sense, a winning combination. This is now the head line more commonly found in a business world dominated and supported by computer technology.

A Sloping Head Line *(6 of Clubs)* reflects a mind that is drawn to the world of fantasy and the imagination, magic, mythology and science fiction. A man with this formation enjoys video games that take him to other worlds and will want to sit through *The Lord of the Rings* many times. His forte is the creative side of business, such as website designer, web artist, or writer. He has one foot on planet earth, and the other foot in the realm of the imagination.

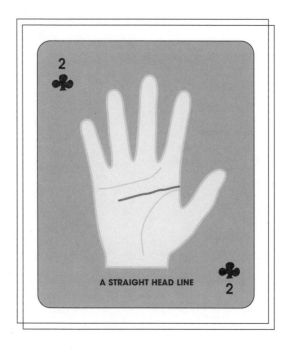

A STRAIGHT HEAD LINE

To make it easier to remember what a Head Line reflects, remember that the top half of the palm is the practical, material world and the bottom half of the palm is the world of the imagination and the unconscious. So whenever you see a Head Line that is predominantly positioned in one or other of these spaces, you know that you have a mind focused on these realms.

Short Head Lines give the ability to see things clearly and concisely while Long Head Lines reflect the tendency to think an issue through. The more curved or undulating a head line, the more flexible and creative the thought processes of its owner.

Finally, if you come across a head line that seems completely

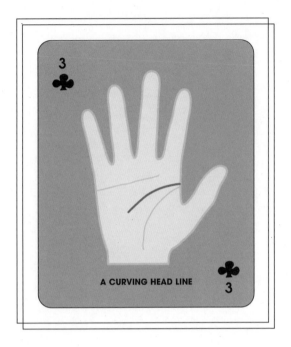

A CURVING HEAD LINE

original (figure 7.2) you can be sure that its owner has an original way of thinking and presenting himself. Perhaps he is eccentric, innovative or outrageously funny, able to find humor where no-one else sees it. He may be a creative genius able to express his originality through the arts. Like the person who has a fingerprint that is unique, the guy with an extraordinary Head Line will have a thought process to match.

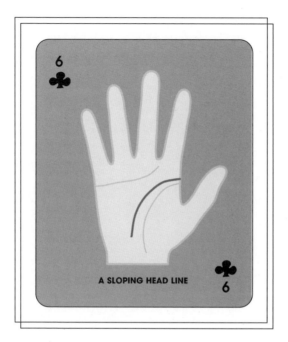

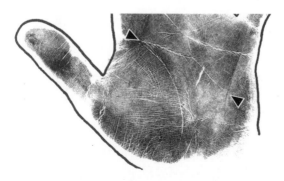

Fig 7.2 *original head line*

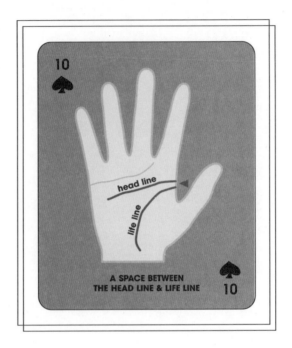

A SPACE BETWEEN HEAD LINE AND LIFE LINE

Impulse control is an important building block towards a successful career and rewarding relationships. A guy who's fearless and risk-taking can seem thrilling and fun. If you're embarking on a career as a trapeze artist, you may want to run an ad for one of these types as your partner. If you're heading to a war zone to make documentaries, you'd do well to find a guy with the moxie to capture award-winning footage and shield you from kidnappers. There are jobs on this planet for almost every known type of character extreme.

But if you're thinking of setting up house with a man who's impulsive and independent, be aware that he's not going to be your average suburban dad, tied to routine. These guys just have to do their own thing. There are features in the hand that reflect the need for independence and the tendency toward impulsiveness.

When there's a wide space between the Head Line and the Life Line *(10 of Spades)* it will be found on an impatient, impulsive guy who likes to make up his mind in a hurry. These men take risks. This gap is found on those who learned to think for themselves at an early age. This probably caused conflict with the parents, especially if mom and dad also had the formation. This wide space shows a broadminded, impulsive and unconventional approach to life.

A small space reflects a person whose independent nature is not going to cause any real angst. But the wider the space, the more extreme the traits it reflects. Someone with this space who has had a falling out with a parent or other family member can turn their back forever without a second thought. He simply forges ahead and gets on with his own life.

In the 1960s, psychologist Walter Mischel gave the "Marshmallow Test" to a group of young children. A teacher took them one by one into a room and showed them a marshmallow on a desk. The child was told that the teacher was leaving but would return in ten minutes. If the child waited, he would get two marshmallows. One child in three could not wait. Mischel kept records of which children gobbled impulsively and which of them waited. He then tracked these kids until they graduated from high school and even beyond. The results were dramatic. He found that the children with self-control were better able to deal with the stresses of daily life. They were confident, trustworthy, self-reliant, and could take the initiative.

Those who had snapped up the marshmallow had veered toward a very different life trajectory. They were more apt to be truant, showed stubborn and indecisive qualities, were easily frustrated, resentful and envious of others, and had short tempers that led to conflict. Even as young adults, they showed that they had not changed from the child who had reached out and grabbed the single marshmallow. They wanted something and they wanted it now.

The patient kids were better students, no matter what their IQ measured. It was obvious that impulse control, or the lack of it, was a predictor of later troubles with authority and the law. When the two groups left school and pursued careers, the differences between them were even greater. By their late twenties, those who had waited were more intellectually skilled, more attentive and better able to concentrate. Perhaps because they were dependable and responsible and had self-control even under difficult circumstances, they developed strong and close relationships.

In contrast, the ones who grabbed the sweet were less mentally adept, less emotionally competent and were often loners. It seemed difficult for them to control their impulsiveness or stick to a path to attain a goal. When under pressure, they would lose control and repeatedly used the same excuses over and over as to why they failed. In their personal lives, the ones who had waited had a better track record and more often ended up in happy, stable marriages.

Other indications of impulsivity in the hand include a short and thick thumb. Short fingers indicate a need to do things quickly, rather than thinking the issues through. And a person who has gaps between all of his fingers, as well as any other indications of impulsivity, will have little compunction about his actions.

HEAD LINE TIED TO THE LIFE LINE

Conversely, when the Head Line is tied to the Life Line *(Jack of*

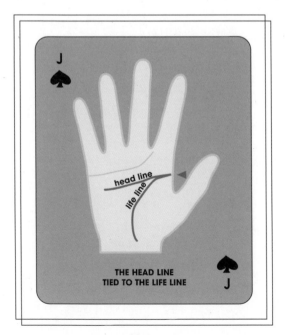

THE HEAD LINE
TIED TO THE LIFE LINE

Spades) at its commencement there is a tendency to be cautious and careful, and the individual will tend to be hesitant to take risks or to commit himself. The more strongly tied these lines, the greater the caution and reluctance to act independently.

These people are tied to their family influence and never veer far from the environment in which they were raised. They may move to another country or marry someone from a different culture, but the chances of these situations remaining stable are not good. If their fingers are held close together this is even more so. This person tends to be more restricted in his outlook than those with a gap between the lines. They're likely to carry on family traditions or repeat the family history.

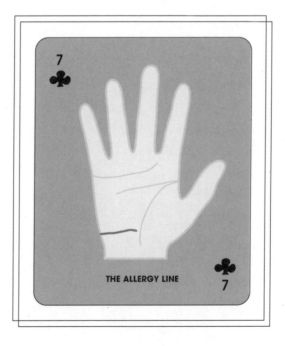

THE ALLERGY LINE

THE ALLERGY LINE

There is a line that can appear at the bottom of the palm called The Allergy Line *(7 of Clubs)*. When found in the hand, the owner has a craving for stimulants of all kinds: chocolate, coffee, alcohol, cigarettes, drugs, sugar, and thrill-seeking. Anyone who has this line will have a history of unusual reactions to such things. Commonly, they either overreact or they underreact to them. They may be allergic to Penicillin or it might take the dentist three shots to successfully numb their gums. They can't have ice cream or Oreos in the house or they'll be gobbled within the hour. If you take these folks to an amusement park, only the biggest, fastest rides appeal to them, and they want to go back five times. Formula One drivers, high-wire artists and drug couriers are some of the people who can have this marking. As can the doctor who dips into his own pharmaceutical supplies and puts six spoons of sugar in his coffee.

The straight form of the line is not as dramatic as when it cuts right across the Life Line (figure 7.3). This is the strongest form of the line with the most powerful effects. There is good news attached to having the Allergy Line. Many people with it become non-smoking, non-drinking vegetarians in their adult years. Having noted their tendency for self-destructive habits, they rein them in. The resulting lifestyle makes it possible that they'll live not only a healthier, but also a longer life than those without the Allergy Line.

This line can come and go in the hand. As you get your habits

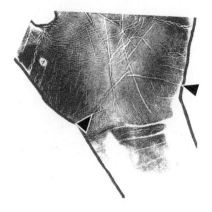

Fig 7.3 *strongest form of allergy line*

under control, you will notice the line breaking down into frag-
ments and almost disappearing. I have the most extreme version
of this line in my hands and have been aware of its effects all
my life. When my daughter, who inherited the Allergy Line, was
young and wired to sugar, I put aside a few days each month
when she was allowed to indulge her sweet tooth. After she grew
up, she confessed that if I had checked more carefully under
her bed, I would have found the discarded wrappers of countless candy bars. Just what my own mother would have found if
she'd gone through my sock drawer.

So the Allergy Line is a blessing in disguise. The downside is
that you wrestle with an attraction to excitement, thrills and bad
habits. The upside is that you become tuned into your body and
health, so much so that eventually you take control and make it
the best it can be. Anyone who has this line in their hand can
take control of their life by limiting their intake of the stimulants that their body is not built to withstand.

CHAPTER EIGHT:

The Thumb—A Miniature Portrait of Its Owner

I f I were asked to read a hand by looking at one single feature, it would be the thumb. When you meet someone for
the first time, take a quick glance at his thumbs. In just a
few seconds, you can gain a snapshot of the man. While there
are exceptions, in general, men have more forcefulness and
willpower and women have more tact and tenacity. You can see
it for yourself when you look at the hands of your male and
female friends. Before we look at the fascinating aspects of the
human thumb, let's examine some of the traits they reflect like
dominance and persuasiveness.

The fact is that no matter how smart and successful a man is,
he can always use the skills and talents that a woman brings to
the table. Take a look at these dynamic couples and think how
different the world would be if they hadn't found each other;
Napoleon and Josephine, John and Jackie Kennedy, Elizabeth
Taylor and Richard Burton, Marie and Pierre Curie, Frida
Kahlo and Diego Rivera, Sonny and Cher, John and Yoko, John
Paul Sartre and Simone de Beauvoir, Robert and Elizabeth
Browning, Lucy and Desi, and Anthony and Cleopatra.

Dominant human beings are more impatient than others due
to their tremendous energy and drive. Modern high-dominance
males work on Wall Street and are found at the head of corpora-
tions. Look around an office, bar or restaurant. Who gets attention the minute he walks in the door? Which guy do the others
defer to? They buy him drinks and offer him a chair but he does
not return the favors.

A dominant man exudes energy and walks with a confident

swagger regardless of his height. He speaks with a resonant voice and looks people in the eye when talking to them. This man likes to call the shots and live by his own rules, get his own way and speak his mind: think of Frank Sinatra, Joseph P. Kennedy, Ernest Hemingway, Pablo Picasso, Aristotle Onassis, Charlie Chaplin, Peter Sellers and many of the men who rule the drug cartels and big business today. If employees call the boss a tyrant you can be sure that he is high dominance. These men who wield an iron fist often leave a trail of broken relationships behind them.

A dominant man can be an outlaw or a hero, a dictator or a saint. Both require many of the same characteristics. There is another type of dominant man who relies more on compromise and co-operation, charm, humor and bargaining techniques to get to the top. These are characteristics of the Alpha Male. Bill Clinton, Gandhi, Che Guevara, Nelson Mandela, Malcolm X, Ronald Reagan, Martin Luther King, Muhammad Ali, Donald Trump, Franklin Roosevelt and Tony Blair are good examples of this type of dominant male. It's interesting to note that all of these men had strong support from capable wives.

Many dominant men in today's world employ techniques like bargaining, compromise, cooperation, and appeals to friendship. In this way they build alliances while still commanding the resources. In other words, they act nice to get what they want. Humans are the only species who have developed language. So it's really no wonder that we have come to the point of manipulating or dominating our fellow man with words. It makes sense that we use everything at our command—money, strength,

courage, social status, even humor— to get others to do our bidding. It's often the way to the top in today's complex technology-
oriented universe.

A man who is very low-dominance has little self-confidence
and would rarely be found in a bar or club. He is bound to his
family and feels most comfortable with close friends. Self-conscious, he finds it hard to accept a compliment, is generally
fearful and easily embarrassed. This guy tends to be moral,
dependable, modest and law-abiding.

Interestingly, though he is different in many ways from the
high-dominance man, the low-dominance man's chances of happiness are about the same. What differs in their unhappiness is
the type of thing they worry about. The low-dominance man
worries over his personality and its shortcomings, his inferiority
feelings and lack of a social life. The high-dominance guy gets
upset about missing a big prize, losing an important client or
controlling his wife's spending habits. In other words, the low-
dominance man is inward-focused and gets eaten up by personal insecurities, whereas the high-dominance man is outward-
focused, looking to other factors as the cause of his misery
because he's generally pretty happy with himself.

A person's dominance can ebb and flow depending on circumstances; as an adolescent, Elvis Presley was shy and did
not stand out at school. He was constantly belittled by other
kids and used his guitar and his powerful voice as a shield.
Once he began to sing publicly and gain acclaim, he blos-
somed. He never really lost his self-deprecating humor and it
became a much-loved part of his adult personality. He accumu-

lated so much power that he never had to raise his voice to get anything that he wanted. Yet he never completely blotted out the early years of shame. And he kept his hometown friends all his life rather than seeking new ones from outside this circle.

There is a pecking order in the animal kingdom, just as there is with human beings. When caged monkeys are offered unlimited amounts of cocaine, it's the ones at the bottom of the pecking order who bang the lever for a steady supply of the white stuff while the dominant animals show a limited interest in the drug. They've already got elevated levels of testosterone, the sexy hormone, and serotonin, the happy hormone, because they're king of the hill, while the subservient males need a leg up. When you have a person like Elvis, who appeared to have everything, and yet ingested as many pills as he is known to have done, you know that he did not feel dominant inside.

Elevated testosterone levels are associated with dominance in men, but only with social dominance, their position in society, and not with physical aggression. A man's success in life brings about high levels of testosterone, which in turn brings on more dominant behavior, which in turn brings more success. Biologists refer to this as "the winner effect". Now you know why the jocks, the school heroes, get the girls.

But a man's testosterone stays high only as long as he is in power. Now you know why rock stars never want to retire. It's not about money, it's about the power that makes them feel alive. And now you understand why highly successful men are often also highly promiscuous. Their testosterone is soaring.

Men can experience a chemical blast from the simple toss of

a coin or from winning at chess. But they must believe that it was their own effort that won the game or there will be no change in their levels of body chemicals. It's such a thrill to be at the Super Bowl when a goal is scored and the fans leap to their feet. There's a collective rush because it's like 10,000 bull moose in heat.

It's not something that men talk about because it's not something they have a great deal of control over. And we know how men hate not feeling in control. The greatest rise and fall of testosterone levels is triggered by a man's relationships with other people, by what is said and done to him. I'm repeating this because it's so important in a marriage. Everything is reflected against his level of self-esteem and then registers as a spike or a dive in his body chemistry. It explains why for many men, social relations are not at the top of their list of things that make him feel like a winner.

THE THUMB IN ALL ITS GLORY

The thumb is vital to establishing the raw material of a man's character. It reflects his ego, willpower, tenacity and energy level. Its size, shape, strength and position on the hand provide a wealth of revealing information. A brief review of the thumb *(Ace of Spades)*: the length indicates how long he holds out in order to reach his goals; the width indicates how much he will push and shove to achieve his heart's desire; the thickness shows whether he favors being blunt or subtle while in pursuit

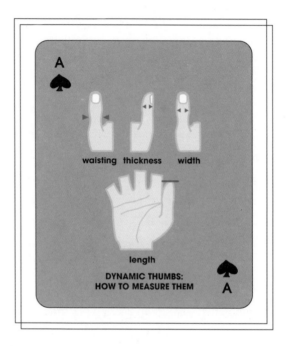

waisting   thickness   width

length

**DYNAMIC THUMBS:
HOW TO MEASURE THEM**

of his dreams. Then there is the interesting aspect known as "waisting," which reflects his tactfulness.

Large Thumbs are found on those with strong personalities and drive. Take a look at any edition of a popular magazine with photos of male celebrities. Then focus on the thumbs. You will find that the quiet, gentle types have more refined and delicate thumbs, whereas the outspoken or boisterous personalities have powerfully formed thumbs. Then look at the hands of any successful politician or businessman and you will see the thumb that is commonly associated with a dominant person.

The more you have the four distinct parts developed, the stronger the character and level of energy. Take a look at the thumbs of any National Hockey League player except the goalie. I have the hand prints of several of these men. Anyone who has the perseverance to come up through the ranks and make it into the big league of professional sports, and then go out onto the ice and body slam another behemoth of a hockey player, will score grade A on almost every aspect of the thumb except for waisting. Yet some of the game's greatest players, such as Wayne Gretzky, do not have enormous thumbs. Wayne has the thumbs of a top business executive, including the gifts of tenacity and diplomacy. His skills of superb skating, visual acuity, and intuition made him a spectacular hockey star.

THE LENGTH OF THE THUMB

When the thumb is held tightly up against the Index Finger, it should come to about two-thirds of the way up the bottom section of that finger *(Ace of Spades)*. This is a good length for a thumb. If it is longer, the person has got an unusual degree of tenacity and perseverance. Nothing will stop them from achieving their goals. If the thumb is also broad, they'll do this in an energetic and forceful manner. If it is thin, they'll pursue success quietly and persistently.

If the thumb falls short of the two-thirds mark, it is considered to be short. Those with a short thumb are impatient and impulsive, the more so the thicker and shorter the thumb. He'll have energy and drive but not much sticking power. If the thumb is both short and thin, the owner will have a great deal of trouble in getting anything accomplished and can be manipulated by those with longer and thicker thumbs. However, if this man has got an outstanding talent, there is no reason why he can't succeed in his chosen field with a good manager behind him.

THE THICKNESS OF THE THUMB

Look at the top joint of his thumb from a sideways perspective *(Ace of Spades)*. If it is thin or flat, he will be gentle rather than forceful, both physically and mentally. The thicker the top portion, the more unfettered he will be in his presentation and dealings. This reflects a man who is driven to succeed and has a blunt manner. If the top tapers off (figure 8.1), he will rely on charm, intellect and gentle persuasion to get what he wants.

When the boss has thick thumbs, you'll know exactly where he stands. He will pursue every avenue if he thinks it will lead him to the top. Don't try to one-up this guy or slack off on the

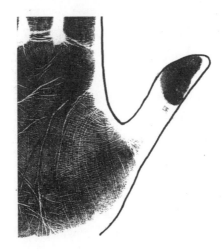

Fig 8.1 *tapering top joint of thumb*

sly. If you don't measure up, he'll let you know in no uncertain terms.

The boss with thin top joints functions differently. He may flatter the staff or throw great parties to gain favor, but you'll have to learn to read him like a book. Because he lacks the forcefulness of Mr. Thick Thumbs, he relies on charm and manners to get the best out of everyone. If he decides to terminate you, he'll ask his secretary to type and deliver your dismissal notice while he's out at lunch.

THE WIDTH OF THE THUMB

The top joint can also be wide *(Ace of Spades)* or it can be narrow as when it's on a Thin Thumb That Looks like a Finger *(9 of Diamonds)*. More often, it is somewhere in between these two widths. Women tend to have thumbs with a narrow to medium top section while men more often measure in the medium to wide range. The width of the top joint is a measure of willpower. It shows how much a person will endure until they achieve their goal. If you hear of someone who suddenly gave up drinking or went cold turkey from a smoking habit, there's a strong likelihood he's got wide top joints.

Such a man will have decisiveness, staying power and the ability to carry out tasks to fruition. In the extreme, it indicates an aggressive nature. When he says he'll deliver the assignment by Friday, it will be there. If he has determined to be the best ballplayer on the team, he will make a great effort to achieve that goal. Conversely, a man with a narrow upper joint may find himself falling behind in his career objectives. He will have to

use other means, such as perseverance and tact, persuasiveness or a natural talent, to gain what other men do through sheer will.

The Thin Thumb that Looks Like a Finger is most commonly found on women. We've already discussed how women use their other skills to out-fox aggressive men. This is basically the formula that men with this thumb formation eventually learn to employ in order to succeed when up against a bully.

THE WAISTED ASPECT OF THE THUMB

When the middle section of the thumb is pinched in, it is referred to as "waisting" *(Ace of Spades)* of the thumb. This

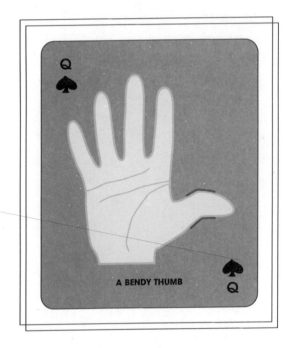

A BENDY THUMB

indicates the presence of tact, diplomacy and persuasiveness. It is commonly found on the thumbs of women and not nearly as frequently on the thumbs of men. If there is little or no waisting, he won't bother with such frivolities as manners or courtesy but will get straight to the point.

Remember the dominant and successful men who used their powers of persuasion and diplomacy? A photo of their hands will show long, strong thumbs with varying degrees of waisting in an impressive hand. By contrast, photos of dominant men who got their way by bullying will feature variations on short and thick thumbs with little or no waisting in powerful hands.

A STIFF OR BENDY THUMB

When you see a man whose thumbs bend back at the middle joint *(Queen of Spades)*, and it's not because he's double-jointed, you can be sure that he is laid-back and adaptable. You don't want the thumb to bend back to an extreme, as though the joint were made of rubber, or you will have someone who is unreliable and with a tendency to procrastination. People with flexible thumbs are cheerful, friendly and easygoing. If they've got a hobby, they rarely get round to finishing projects, but don't really care. This man has to concentrate on the task-at-hand if he is self-employed because he can lack persistence. He could do well in the arts if he has a particular gift.

The man with stiff thumbs *(King of Spades)* will be stubborn,

STIFF THUMBS

reliable, and responsible but can have difficulty adapting to new ideas and unexpected developments. He's the guy for you if perseverance and dependability are what you seek. While the bendy thumbed man is adaptable, the stiff thumbed guy will tend to stick to the tried and true, and he'll hammer away until the task is done, with no pit stops for beer or football on the way. Those with stiff thumbs are the worker bees of the world.

THE CLUBBED THUMB

This rare formation is dramatic when you see it for the first time (figure 8.2). The nail as well as the whole top joint of the thumb is very wide and short and thick. It looks almost swollen.

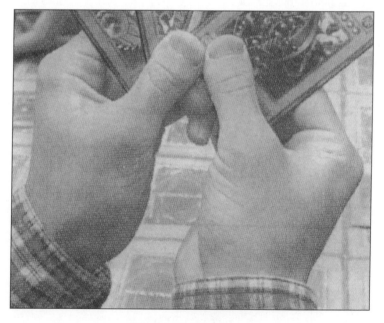

Fig 8.2 *clubbed thumb*

Anyone who has this type of thumb will undergo bouts of explosive emotion. It might be an ocean of tears or a temper tantrum. These fits can take the person by surprise because they don't realize why they are reacting so violently. It usually occurs when they are being shamed or taunted and their unconscious triggers a memory that sets them off.

All of us can have crying jags or emotional upsets when someone opens an old emotional wound. But for those with a Clubbed Thumb, it seems that they have a particularly difficult time keeping the anger from boiling over. Perhaps the body chemistry causes the unusual shape and the emotional reaction. If you're around a man with clubbed thumbs, take great care not to insult him or have him take offence at an offhand remark, no matter how innocently intended.

A QUICK SNAPSHOT

Now you can glance at the hands of anyone and quickly ascertain many things about their character. By assessing the length, width and thickness of their thumbs, and then checking to see if there is any waisting, you have a quick snapshot. Depending on what you're looking for, whether a business partner or an intimate friend, you can now make the decision as to whether you want to get to know this person better. If there is waisting, you can feel free to approach them. If the top section is thick and wide, you will know to engage all of your persuasive talents in order to tackle this tough cookie successfully. If you're staring at a thin, small digit, you might want to head for the exit, unless you need a gentle talk with a sympathetic soul who doesn't often get the chance to socialize. Whatever your needs, a quick look at a person's thumbs prepares you to handle him or her with confidence.

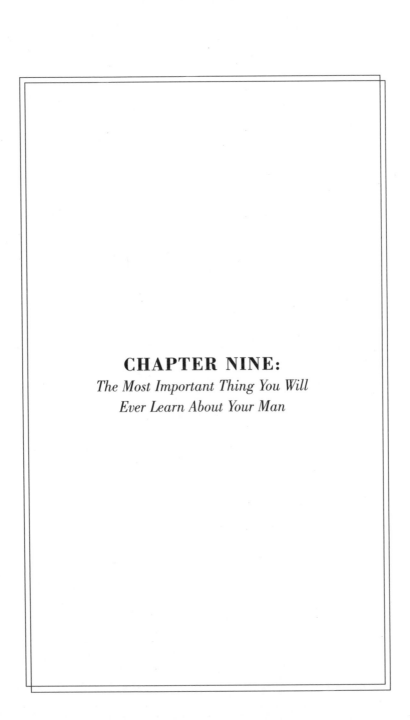

CHAPTER NINE:
The Most Important Thing You Will
Ever Learn About Your Man

THE SECRET REVEALED

My observation of hands and human behavior points to astonishing evidence that *nearly half* of all men suffer from some degree of shyness or ego inhibition. This is one of the best-kept secrets about men because they are so loathe to admit any sort of vulnerability. This shyness is reflected by their Index Fingers, which range from just a little short to very short. How they feel about themselves and how this affects their personal relationships is directly connected to the length of this digit.

All men are vulnerable, of course—but those who were born shy feel the pain of rejection more deeply and hold onto it longer. Men need to feel comfortable with who they are and hate being told to change. Men have been taught to "act like a man" since they could toddle and they've got their pride tied up in the results. When you consider that men are evaluated by society largely by the degree to which they fit a masculine ideal, you see why they can never afford to lose one drop of the ground they fought so hard to gain. A man's ego is tied directly to his masculinity. My study of hands shows that as many as half of all men feel they are on very shaky ground here.

Many men don't realize that being born shy is an inherited trait and that it is causing the havoc in their lives. This may be because it remains a taboo subject. Several American psychologists are pursuing serious studies of the phenomenon of being born shy. But try to find a man on the street that would agree to go on television and admit to being shy.

I keep records of major changes in the lives of my clients. Because I have their handprints, I've been able to check these for the possible cause of incidents. I made a surprising discovery about the Index Finger. Taking a random pick of eighty men and women from a wide range of ages and income, I saw that they divided into two neat halves. There were those with Average Index Fingers, and those with a variation of the Short Index Finger. As I ran down the second list, I saw that the Short Index Fingers were my "born shy" clients. They had the more colorful lives, sometimes riddled with upheaval. Many had achieved fame or gained recognition in their field. A significant number had divorced. Here is my tally:

	BORN SHY (28 MEN/12 WOMEN)	NOT BORN SHY (15 MEN/25 WOMEN)
Drug Problem	50%	8%
Alcohol Problem	40%	5%
Workaholic	30%	0%
Sex Addiction	10%	0%
Suicide Attempts	20%	0%
Attained Fame and Recognition	32%	3%
Divorced	60%	12%
Self-Employed	70%	25%
No Major Problems	5%	90%

Although I'd read many books on being born shy, I'd never seen a more dramatic look at real lives. The first thing I noticed is that there are more men who are born shy than there are women.

And though I knew that being born shy does not sentence a person to a life of emotional trauma and loneliness, it seemed that it inclined them to be prone to more of the above behaviors. Certainly it makes social relations more difficult and social relations are the key to our emotional health and welfare. Recent research shows that having a diverse social network may boost the immune system.

It's important to keep in mind that being born shy can spur a person on to fame and fortune because they are prone to making a greater effort. Many of the world's outstanding artists, statesmen and achievers started life as shy individuals and fought valiantly to prove themselves: Andy Warhol, John Lennon, Martin Scorsese, James Dean, Jim Carrey, Frank Sinatra, Miles Davis, Kurt Cobain, Sly Stallone, George Clooney, David Bowie, Russell Crowe, Muhammed Ali, Robert de Niro, Elvis Presley, Prince, and Malcolm X. Photographs of the hands of these people show them to have Short or Very Short Index Fingers.

Many shy men manage to marry and, for them, being married is an anchor. Yet too often these marriages fail. That is why I am letting the women who love them in on the secrets of their inner world. Even if your partner was not born shy, there will be many men in your life who are and who would be grateful for your compassion. Men don't like to talk about, much less have pointed out, anything about them that can be perceived as a weakness. If this can be stated for all men, then it is more poignantly true for those who were born shy.

Keeping in mind what you have learned about men so far, try to imagine how a guy who was born shy reacts to criticism. It's only natural for a woman to be proud of the man in her life. So when she sees him as less than she would like him to be, there are going to be words. "Pull-ease!" when he shows up in an old t-shirt with beer stains. "You're just like your father!" always goes down well. Anything acerbic that rolls off her tongue will do the trick. A man with an Average Index Finger can forget the remarks in ten minutes, let them bounce right off him, or even give her back better than she gave him. But the man with a Short Index Finger, especially if he also has a Loop of Serious Intent, hears her words and thinks they may be true, becomes angry and then wonders why she's even with such a loser. He'll toss and turn all night and, if the index fingers are really short, may dream of revenge.

THE WORLD OF THE SHY

There are still strong taboos in the 21st Century for all of us. Men don't easily reveal how much they earn or how they spend it because they are judged by their income. They live in a sex-saturated world yet it's hard for most to say "I love you". Their job means more to them than you can imagine.

What men fear most in life is being rejected, scorned and tossed aside. If they admit they're low-income, tell a woman they love her, make a fool of themselves on the dance floor, or lose their job, they put themselves at risk of being shamed in front of others. For the man who is born shy, this fear lies too close to the surface for comfort. He must constantly keep it at bay. A confident man can certainly experience shame, but he is quicker to bounce back with the help of his ego. When someone tosses off an insult, he looks at who dished it out and then gets over it. The shy man absorbs the words and fears they may be true.

If human identity depends on other people, on how we see ourselves reflected in their eyes, then the self-image of a shy person can only be poor. Not only do they feel insecure and inadequate, but even when they receive praise they doubt its sincerity. Self-doubt eats at the core of the soul. So the very ones who desperately need to look others in the eye and see that they are valued, cannot do that simple thing, for fear of what they might see. This self-doubting mechanism is a trick of the mind and has little to do with reality. But if you've been exposed to negative input from childhood, it becomes an automatic reflex.

Angelina Jolie and Billy Bob Thornton met on a film set in Toronto. They fell head over heels in love and eventually married. I took a look at their hands in magazine photos and saw that the newlyweds were not going to have an easy time. Angelina was born with confidence and has sustained it into her adult years. She was fortunate to have been born with a healthy ego to help her through her parents' divorce and the loss of a father in her life. Billy Bob, on the other hand, was born hypersensitive and had a difficult childhood with a brutal father.

The characteristics associated with someone who has a Long Index Finger like Angelina, and those of someone whose Index Finger is Short like that of Billy Bob, are very different. Angelina is fearless and can travel anywhere at the drop of a hat, speaking with ease to anyone she meets on the way. Billy Bob feels most comfortable in a known environment, with family or long-standing friends, and would be reluctant to strike out for places unknown that are filled with strangers. Though we are talking specifically about geographic travel, it could as easily apply to psychological conditions, to something as simple as changing his home or his regular routine on a Saturday night.

So we have Angelina the great explorer and hardy soul, married to Billy Bob, the sensitive and reticent soul. He may be talented, smart, caring and funny as hell, but he can't go where Angelina dares to tread without the risk of feeling the fear that inexplicably wells up inside of him. Walking in her luminescent shadow rather than by her side as an equal seems to be what prompted him to abandon the marriage. It had nothing to do with his genuine love for this woman, though Angelina may not be aware of this. She would only have seen the consequences, the drifting apart and the divorce. It's not easy for a confident person to put herself into the shoes of the shy. It is only human to look at surface behavior and to misinterpret his fears as a lack of interest.

In an interview with Bob Costas, Billy Bob said his relationship with his father was difficult, that he got very nervous as a kid when he knew that his father would soon be home. This tal-

ented actor feels that all of the insecurities in his life spring
from the fact that his dad never told him he was okay. If Billy
Bob had been born bolder, he could have let his father's nega-
tivity roll off his back. Yet this sensitivity, while making his
romantic relationships difficult, has assuredly contributed to his
superlative gifts as an actor and writer. This is the story of so
many of the world's great artists.

The very essence of maleness and masculinity is defined by
the strong and positive vocabulary that is aligned with the word
confidence.

But my study of hands has shown that there are more shy men
than women. Shyness is seen as a weakness if found in a male
who lives in a culture like North America that values rugged
individualism, dominance and courage. Yet shy people are some
of the most courageous persons I have ever known, when you
consider that being born shy predisposes a person to feel and do
many of the following:

- Lack self-confidence and doubt their own abilities
- Fear failure and constantly search for acceptance
- Prefer to be self-employed
- Feel uneasy with strangers and authority figures
- Constantly worry they won't "measure up"
- Repeat a task over and over in search of "perfection"
- Anticipate criticism and react badly when it occurs
- Experience difficulty in accepting or believing a compliment
- Be seen as an easy target by unscrupulous people
- Feel like the outsider or loner in any group

•Search for a "buzz" to overcome depression and pessimism

•Hold a grudge and dream of revenge when slighted

•Get to the top of the ladder; attain fame

The important thing to keep in mind about being shy is that it is not *you*, it is only how you *think* you are. A shy person needs to constantly remind himself that he is not inferior to anyone. His bad feelings are just a trick of the mind, the by-product of a sensitive nature that makes him doubt himself. With a shy person, his conscious mind is so finely attuned to a perceived insult or potential harm that it constantly triggers his unconscious mind.

Perhaps the most painful part of being shy is being misunderstood or misread. A person who can't look others in the eye or who keeps silent when asked a question is often labeled a snob or thought to be stand-offish. This couldn't be further from the truth. Shy people would give their right arm to take part in an easy, amiable conversation with their peers. But they are so self-conscious, always expecting the worst to come out of their mouth, and so afraid to push themselves forward into the limelight for fear of public failure, that they end up doing the safest thing, which is to remain silent, eyes down. There is no doubt that chronic shyness is one road to pessimism, because shy people often miss out on opportunities and then berate themselves for not having tried.

INFLUENCES AND EFFECTS

There are many factors to consider when looking into the heart of the man you love. In her book, *The Nurture Assumption*, Judith Rich Harris says researchers have found that a child's attractiveness determines how people treat him. A mother pays more attention to her baby if the child is cute. Good-looking babies are looked at more, played with more and given more affection than unattractive ones. If they do something wrong, the Plain Janes are punished more harshly than the pretty girls. If they don't do anything wrong, people are quicker to think that they did. Plain children and beautiful children grow up in different worlds, even in the same family. Being shy on top of being plain makes life even harder. Mothers can have patience with their timid children but fathers often express disgust and have little patience with a son who is not bold and brave.

Hope and optimism are two of the most powerful forces for happiness in any human life. Having hope means not giving in to anxiety, or a defeatist attitude, or depression in the face of challenges and setbacks. Optimism means having a strong expectation that everything will turn out okay, despite frustrations. Many shy people cling to hope like a drowning person to a lifebuoy, even though being optimistic is more difficult for them due to their self-doubt mechanism. There are so many famous and accomplished men who were born shy that I've concluded it's one of the greatest catalysts for driving a man to fame. It makes him take whatever ability he possesses and push for success, possibly so that he can show the bullies who taunted him that he is not a loser.

A shy person is often smarter and more sensitive than other folks. The shy child tends to stand on the sidelines as an observer. Because he is taunted, his condition becomes exacerbated, but at the same time he becomes an expert on human nature. He may retreat into a fantasy world in order to escape the harshness of reality. But because he has been exposed to so much at such a young age, he often grows up to be more knowledgeable and caring than those who had an easy childhood and who coasted through on their looks or charm. Learning to act is one way to deal with being shy. Many of the world's greatest performers hide an innately timid soul beneath the exterior they have learned to project as though it were a second, and protective, skin.

Eric Clapton was a child who knew the torment of being unwanted. Yet this man took his inner pain and fused it to creative genius. Eric, a brilliant blues guitarist, has been off drugs for many years, but estimates that he spent millions of dollars on getting high to escape his sense of inferiority.

Clapton was the first-born son of a fifteen-year-old English girl and a Canadian soldier, whose mother gave birth to him during a black-out in World War II. His mother deserted Eric when he was two and moved overseas. He grew up believing that his grandparents were his parents. When Eric was twelve, his mother returned briefly and told him the truth. When he found out he was illegitimate, he wanted the ground to open up and swallow him. At school, he became angry and withdrawn.

Alone in his bedroom, he practiced the guitar obsessively. His short index fingers reflect the fact that Eric was born shy.

As a young musician, Clapton went down the path of drugs and alcohol. Undoubtedly, these gave him "courage." With marriages and a string of women behind him, he says he has many problems with his sexuality, which all tie up with the resentment he felt toward his mother when he was younger. He blamed her for abandoning him. Then one day he woke up and realized that he was doing the same thing to his girlfriends as his mother had done to him.

Few people who saw Eric perform during his long career would have guessed that he lacked self-confidence. The alcohol and drugs masked his anxiety. But they didn't fool Eric and he eventually got sober. He now spends his time raising millions for a drug rehab program called *Crossroads* that he started in Antigua. Undoubtedly this humanitarian gesture gives him a warm buzz and increases his self-worth, things he once tried to find in drugs and alcohol.

British author Colin Wilson says that shyness is a disinclination to express oneself out of fear that things will turn out badly, whereas confidence is the ability to act decisively. A man who is fearful is seen as weak and unreliable and probably of no help in times of trouble, a man who is confident is seen as strong and in control. No wonder shy men like Eric reach for a drink or other chemical that can strip away their inhibitions. But then, addiction wrecks their lives.

In the final chapter you are going to find out how to gauge whether your man was born with a degree of shyness and whether he overcame it.

Remember that of all the important features in the hand, none has the same impact on a man's life and potential happiness as the *strength of his ego*. Your understanding of this feature can be incorporated into everything else this book teaches you about him. The ego acts as a sort of conduit through which so much of a man's personality and behavior get filtered. It is the catalyst for most of his words and actions. As you've learned, even fame and fortune don't ease the self-doubt that can flood through a man who was born shy. Understanding this will help you to alleviate misunderstandings and smooth the way to a more loving and rewarding relationship for you both. Once you measure your own and your partner's Index Fingers as featured in the final chapter, you may see the relationship from a fresh perspective.

CHAPTER TEN:

The Key to Successful Relationships

A lthough a man's thumb gives you a quick overview of important traits, the Index Finger allows you to see how he feels about himself. This digit is a reflection of his self-confidence. Our sense of self is pivotal to our thoughts, actions, words, ambitions, feelings and outlook on life. These are all intertwined, since it is the brain that triggers our emotions and it is our emotions that principally guide us in our dealings with others. On this one digit hinges so much more.

All men experience testosterone highs and lows. So all men feel less than wonderful when they are criticized or seen to fail. Check the faces of players after a big game. The camera zooms in on the winners, who are ecstatic. They may be on their knees, hands raised, or wildly hugging other players. Scientists know that winners of a competition experience an abrupt surge in testosterone that lasts for up to twenty-four hours. But when the camera pans to a guy on the losing team, there is a sad, blank stare. The body is still, his chemicals in a nosedive that won't get back to base level for days.

Men experience these feelings on a daily basis, according to how they perceive they have performed. The guys on the losing team with Short Index Fingers suffer the most. They will mull over the events that led up to the loss, going over them obsessively, which only serves to further upset them. It will take a long time to forget the game and feel good again. Players with Average Index Fingers will shrug off the loss and think about winning the next game. They won't beat themselves up with all the "What if's" and "If only's" that can plague those with shorter index fingers.

There are three main lengths for an Index Finger. It can be *Long* or it can be *Average* or it can be *Short*. Because up to half of all men were born with a degree of shyness you have a fifty percent chance of marrying one of them. Look at the index finger on his passive hand. This is the hand that directly registers how he felt about himself as a child. Then, to see how he has dealt with life, look at the index finger on his dominant hand. Some men, depending on their looks, life experiences and efforts, manage to mask the early anxieties. Yet they are never totally free of its effects because of the power of the unconscious mind.

THE SHORT INDEX FINGER

We've covered a great deal about being born shy which is reflected by a Short Index Finger *(6 of Diamonds)*. For the women who marry these men, this information influences every aspect of his character and behavior. Therefore it is the essential key to making a relationship with these men work by avoiding the misunderstandings that can easily occur due to the taboos associated with being born male and shy.

The Short Index Finger is anything that measures shorter than half-way down the top joint of the Middle Finger. It indicates a degree of self-doubt that can lead to a lack of self-confidence. This, in turn, makes life more difficult. It takes tremendous

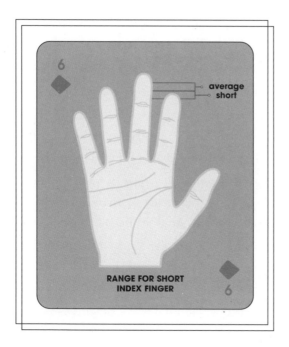

average
short

RANGE FOR SHORT
INDEX FINGER

effort and willpower to learn to cope with these feelings and to hide them from the world.

There are more shy men than women. This is partly due to the fact that many girls who were born shy overcame it. Women are more emotionally competent and socially skilled than men. They have both the ability and the opportunity to deal with their innate sensitivity. Men simply learn to mask it. It becomes a Catch-22 for men because being shy makes them anxious and being anxious makes them more self-conscious about their shyness.

Because of anxiety in the workplace—the boss, other employees and the demands of the job itself—self-employment is a good choice for shy people. In an environment where they are in control, there are fewer instances for stress or failure. Short Index Finger people can thrive when they start up their own business because they tend to work hard and are driven to succeed. Working in the arts or as a performer can also pay off. Some Short Index Finger people go into politics and make a success of it. Their self-doubt acts as a catalyst to push them into a position of power and control where nobody can ever criticize or hurt them again. Ariel Sharon and Vladimir Putin have this finger formation. Their Short Index Fingers are found in powerful hands reflecting abilities that helped them get to the top.

A politician with a Short Index Finger will always react sharply to any kind of criticism, even seeing it where it does not exist. They always want to be right. By contrast, such leaders as Ronald Reagan, Jimmy Carter and Bill Clinton, with their Average Index Fingers, engaged in calm debate when attacked, without flying off the handle. So the psychological predisposition to self-doubt, as reflected by a Short Index Finger, can cause emotional upset, even while it pushes the owner to achieve in an effort to get above all criticism.

Jim Carrey was born painfully shy, as were many of our greatest comedians. The first acceptance they felt as youngsters was often the sound of laughter coming from family and friends. When you look at their lives you can be sure that fame and fortune were never the main goal. Money is good, and provides a sense of security, but it was not the impetus that drove this person. As for the fame, for those who are fueled by self-doubt, there can never be enough. They suck up those spotlights and applause like they are the breath of life.

Because those with Short Index Fingers constantly worry that they might fail, they work hard to keep their skills honed and tend to be perfectionists. In other words, they are excellent employees in many ways. And it's not that they lack people skills, but rather that they are so hypersensitive to any comment that it gets in the way of their personal and work relationships. For example, you can't make a jest about lateness to a Short Index Finger guy or he will think you are going to turn him in to the boss. This is particularly the case if he also has a Loop of Serious Intent.

Those with a Short Index Finger not only anticipate criticism, they actually expect it. The shorter this finger, the more reluctant the owner will be to ask for directions when lost, or help when he needs it. He will do anything not to risk the shame of being seen as less than competent, less than a man. These people were born hyper-reactive to strange people and situations. The way they appear on the outside, with their shocked expression or blank stare, is not at all how they are feeling inside. These sensitive individuals are often mis-read by others when they have simply gone blank with fear. Ironically, their most common fears are of being criticized or misunderstood!

I have said before that you can't change a man, but you can change the way you respond to him so that you both benefit. Now that you've had an in-depth look at how a man's ego affects his life, I hope it will help you to empathize with your man.

Short Index Finger men have a short fuse, simply because they often see criticism even where it was not meant. It takes courage to tell your partner in a calm and caring voice how much his angry words affect you. But such words will help to build the bridge of empathy and understanding from which flows love.

It takes patience to live with a person who is filled with self-doubt. At the same time, these people are among the most fascinating, lively, sensitive and caring individuals you may ever have in your life. So don't ever turn away from them because of what you see on the surface. What you have to do is find a way to gain his trust, and then his love will follow. And you can be his rock.

Johnny Cash was born shy and fought a pitched battle to overcome it all of his life. He found his soul mate when he fell in love with and married June Carter Cash. In his autobiography, *Cash*, Johnny talked about his struggles and how June was always there for him, helping him get through.

He described how he took his first amphetamine while on tour and how he loved it. The pills increased his energy, sharpened his wit and banished his shyness. They also improved his timing and made him feel almost electrified. He confessed that he had no problem being on stage in front of ten thousand strangers, but fell into awkwardness when backstage with only ten. He had the greatest praise for his beloved wife, June, who would hold his hand at such times and lessen his anxiety by dealing with the visitors.

There are many shy men who are loving and stable, who have

found a safe harbor in life like Johnny Cash did. I suggest that a strong marriage can be that harbor, even if it is filled with challenge. Having a partner who understands the roots of a sensitive nature is vital.

THE LONG INDEX FINGER

The Long Index Finger *(5 of Diamonds)* is anything measuring higher than two-thirds of the way up the top joint of the Middle Finger. While it might suggest that its owner is filled with confidence and won't suffer the way a Short Index Finger person can, it's not that simple. For starters, there are far more women with

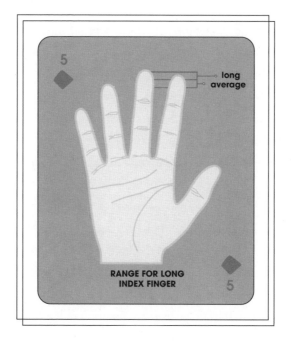

207

Long Index Fingers than there are men. Why is not known, though it may be hormonal in origin. Some women readers will find that they have this form of the index finger. Because it reflects characteristics that extend beyond the average range, it is just as important to know about as the Short Index Finger.

The shorter the Short Index Finger, the more extreme the associated behavior, just as the longer the Long Index Finger, the more intense the associated qualities. Most of the world's top models have Long Index Fingers, as do some politicians: Margaret Thatcher, Fidel Castro, Hillary Clinton, plus movie stars Nicole Kidman, Greta Garbo, Angelina Jolie, Bette Davis, Joan Crawford, Madonna, etc. Ironically, more male movie stars have Average or Short Index Fingers than Long ones. This causes ego clashes in many Hollywood marriages. If you look at the few long-standing romances in Tinseltown, it is almost always the case that the wife is not in show business. Or if she is, she put her career aside to be a wife and mother. No Long Index Finger person would be happy in such a situation unless they could influence the power behind the throne.

A Long Index Finger reflects a strong ego or sense of self. The owner will be quite sure of his abilities and enjoy getting to the top. In fact, he expects to get to succeed in whatever business he has chosen simply because it just never occurs to him that he should remain an underling. He can take the lead with no qualms and set a confident example for those who follow. Rather than suffering from nerves like the Short Index Finger, this guy is smooth as glass.

You could say that these men are natural leaders, rather than

leaders who climbed up in an attempt to bury insecurities. The
Long Index Finger man takes control of his own affairs and is
not easy for others to influence. He needs to be boss. Donald
Trump is an excellent example, a born entrepreneur with a long
index finger. You can tell him he won't have a snowball's
chance in hell of winning an election and he'll go right ahead
and campaign confidently. And people respond to his confidence. You cannot threaten him. He wears his confidence as a
sort of armor plating that deflects any negative comment.

Sometimes you can find a Long Index Finger person who says
he is shy or introverted or insecure. This is not the case. He is
mistaking his own preoccupation with his self-image for self-
doubt. These are poles apart. This guy appears to others to be
supremely confident and self-possessed. He always has an opinion and is never shy about voicing it. And whatever the topic of
conversation may be, just listen to how often it drifts back to his
accomplishments and his life. These men are proud and can be
good leaders if they have other skills and abilities. But most of
all they are absorbed with their own sense of self and endlessly
ask questions such as "Where am I going?" "Was that the best
decision for my career?" and that old perennial, "What about
me?"

Those with Long Index Fingers want to be respected and
admired by others. They don't really care if you like them.

It's not wise to make fun of a Long Index Finger person. They
are not into the self-deprecating school of humor. In fact,
remember how the Short Index Finger person tends to see criticism even where it does not exist? Well, the Long Index Finger

person takes everything so seriously that it can appear that the same mechanism is at work. It is not. He simply mulls over every word you say and makes sure that it truly reflects the way he sees himself, in the best light possible. The Sun sign closest to the Long Index Finger is Leo, ruled by the Sun and represented by the king of the jungle. Because they tend to be serious and hardworking, they see no reason why the very top shouldn't be their place in the natural order of things.

Long Index Finger people hate to be told what to do. After all, they've spent considerable time thinking about their strengths and shoring up their weak spots, and consider that they know best. So why should anyone else pass judgment on them? The only thing that stands between them and getting elected to head any group is that a few deadweights with Short Index Fingers felt slighted by what they perceived to be condescension in the campaign speeches. The Average Index Finger folks have no problem with the Long Index Fingers and are rushing up to cast their ballots for them.

As I mentioned, there are many more women who have a long index than men. It's interesting to note that many young women these days are wearing rings on their index finger. This was once quite rare. Wearing a ring on this digit gives a boost to the owner's sense of self. In a way, it's almost like extending the index finger so that it is longer. This trend to wear rings on digits that are both associated with the ego, such as the thumb and the index finger, may be due to the modern pressures on a young woman to succeed and to act self-confident. Wearing a ring on a certain finger gives comfort and puts emphasis on the related area of your life.

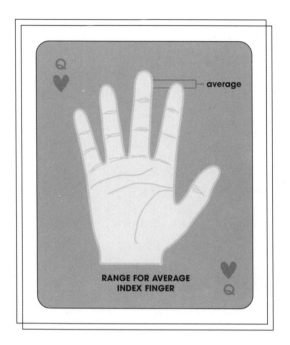

THE AVERAGE INDEX FINGER

The Average Index Finger *(Queen of Hearts)* is anything that measures between halfway and two-thirds up the top joint of the Middle Finger. If your man has got this formation he is fortunate. It indicates that he was born with a good measure of confidence when found in his passive hand and that he is relaxed with himself when in his dominant hand. This man can withstand criticism and challenge with more ease than other men. He has a protective layer that was there at birth. He tends to throw off adversity with few scars remaining. It is a great gift, though he may not be aware of it.

Now let's look at the final formations associated with the index finger. Like those we've just discussed, these pertain to a man's sense of self and are a direct reflection of the state of his ego.

THE INDEX FINGER STICKING OUT

Sometimes a person holds their Index Finger Sticking Out *(7 of Diamonds)*. This most often happens when a person has a degree of shyness. It indicates a strong effort to overcome self-doubt. In fact, what you get when you find this formation is a

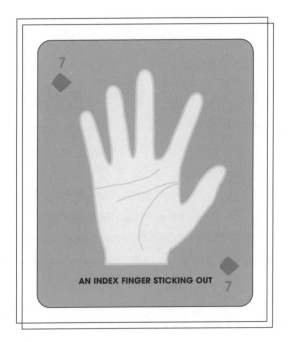

AN INDEX FINGER STICKING OUT

person who tends to go overboard in their presentation. They are pushing themselves forward to mask their anxiety. It's actually a very successful ploy.

If the finger is Average Length and sticking out, it reflects a mild extroversion. This is a temporary finger position. It reflects the fact that the owner is in a stressful period of his life and is asserting himself more than usual. If the finger is Short and sticking out, which is more common, you will have a person who is attempting to bury all the self-doubt. This formation can be a permanent one when the finger is short. Many salesmen have a Short Index Finger Sticking Out and can deliver a rapid spiel without drawing breath for the customer's comments.

If you've fallen in love with a man who has this formation, you can point all of this out to him. He will be amazed, especially if his index finger is short, because he has been acting the extrovert for so long that he may have forgotten he was born shy! However, if you describe the traits as outlined in this book he will tell you that it's an accurate portrait. Remember that it's very difficult for any of us to be objective about how we appear to others. But we all feel thrilled when someone takes the time to let us know just how we come across, especially if they speak to us with respect, tact and constructive commentary about the possibility that our personal lives can run smoother.

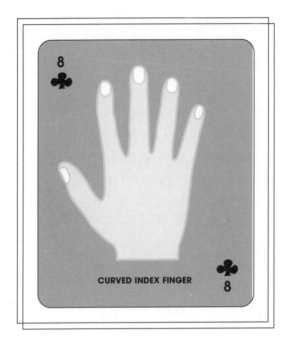

CURVED INDEX FINGER

A CURVED INDEX FINGER

When the Index Finger Curves inward *(8 of Clubs)* toward the Middle Finger, it's an indication of insecurity rather than self-doubt. This is most commonly expressed by the instinct to collect things. People with this formation can be found in junk shops, bidding nervously at auctions, browsing through thrift shops and buying secondhand books that they don't need. It is not the acquisition of the object for its own sake that is at work here, but rather the need for a security blanket that finds them on this constant search. Anyone can be a collector for all kinds of reasons and they can have any sort of index finger formation. But when you find a Curved Index Finger, you always have a person who collects specifically for the sense of security that it bestows.

This finger began to curve inward in the early years. It reflects an uneasy or insecure childhood. Perhaps there was a sibling bully or an aggressive parent who made life seem very unpredictable. Even as a child, the Curved Index Finger person will accumulate cards, dinosaurs or stamps at a fierce rate and protect them with his life. Again, he is not so much fascinated by stamps from Fiji as he is drawing a safe cloak around his person to keep out the embattled world that seems to overwhelm him.

A WORD ABOUT WOMEN WITH SHORT INDEX FINGERS

It's sometimes asked, "Why do nice girls end up with bastards?" If you look at her hands, you're likely to find a Short Index Finger on one or both of them. Because of the self-doubt mechanism, the nice girl does not look out for her own best interests. It may be that she married the first reasonable man who asked her, because she feared that nobody else would have her. Or she could have continued to date a disreputable beau long after another woman would have dropped him like a hot potato. If she has gotten involved with a man who is manipulative – and it's true that such men can spy an overly sensitive woman a block away – she probably can't bring herself to leave him. When you're filled with self-doubt, you blame yourself and rationalize to give the other person the benefit of the doubt.

So for the woman with a Short Index Finger, either on the passive hand or on both hands, it is paramount that she focuses on finding a man who is worthy of her and who is not a predator. She may want to write a list of features she is looking for in a husband and carry it around and read it regularly. Then, when she does meet someone and has been out with him a few times, she can check off how he measures up. If he falls short, it would be a good idea to let him slide, no matter how strong the physical attraction. Keep in mind that women tend to be attracted to higher dominance men, but a very high dominance man is too aggressive for most women with Short Index Fingers. And a man with Long Index Fingers needs to be boss, period.

What is suitable for her? A man with Average Index Fingers and otherwise compatible hands can be a good husband for any woman, regardless of her index finger length. But it's also true that a shy woman is particularly drawn to shy men. They have an empathetic bond that can result in a very powerful love affair. As long as they are aware that some problems may arise due to the effects of being born hypersensitive, and as long as they keep the gates of compassion and communication wide open, they can have a very powerful union.

WHAT ABOUT MARRYING MEN WITH SHORT INDEX FINGERS?

It's also said that "nice guys end up with the bitches." Again, you can be sure that a fair number of men who are bossed around by their wives have a Short Index Finger and their wives' fingers are longer. Even tremendous good looks can't convince some men that they are really special, and they can end up marrying for the same wrong reasons as the shy woman. Then they stay too long in unhappy unions, fearing change. They'd be lucky indeed to marry someone who adores them, rather than one that puts them down.

Men with Short Index Fingers are born hyper-reactive and are much more sensitive to the world at large than those born with confidence. They get emotional over things that other guys would simply disregard, such as a casual remark they take badly or the fear that they have not done well at work. This explains why these men also work harder than anyone else to be the best they can in order to avoid criticism. In fact, they are often the world's greatest achievers, except in marriage.

It's sad to say, but a man with Short Index Fingers is the least likely candidate to get through life without being divorced at least once. He may even end up alone by choice. This is due to the fact that the wear and tear of ordinary life, while somewhat of a cakewalk for those who have Average or Long Index Fingers, can be a minefield for a man who was born shy. He has a greater chance of attaining success or notoriety than the others, but not an equal chance of sustaining a happy marriage. Think about the potential for nagging that could crop up with a guy who grunts rather than answers your questions, who calms his anxiety with whiskey, and who may be a workaholic but have no idea as to why.

Who is a suitable partner for him? And is he really a good marriage prospect? I think that he can be a wonderful partner for a sensitive woman who can see into his soul and forgive some of the emotional upsets that occur. Life is more complicated for a man with Short Index Fingers than for a woman with this feature. She has the possibility of being a stay-at-home mom, and she'll be a great one. This is a form of self-employment and it takes a lot of the pressure of working in the outside world off her. But men—even in this day and age—rarely have such choices.

If he commutes to work every day and then returns at night, he may stop off for a few martinis before the train leaves. Just thinking back over events at the office can raise his blood pressure. And knowing what's in store for him at the other end - did he pick up the Pampers and prosciutto? Or was it the Charmin and corned beef? His head is pounding already trying to get it straight. "Make it a double, bartender!" He wants to calm those nerves because God forbid he should look like a fool in front of his own kids.

And so it goes, in an unending symphony of self-abuse. For the man with the Short Index Fingers, life was never meant to be easy. And it is not. He spends a good deal of his time building up walls to keep out the self-doubt demons. And those walls can become a barrier in his most intimate relationships, bringing heartbreak through misunderstandings. His children and even his wife can easily misinterpret his actions and words, which often spring from his unconscious mind. Because that is where our emotions lie, and the emotions from the childhood of a shy boy are always intense and often defensive. Yet this man desperately wants to love and be loved, possibly more so than the man with Average Index Fingers, who is not consumed by the same degree of worry, loss and sorrow.

The man with Short Index Fingers will find his most empathetic partner in a woman who was also born shy. She may have an Average Index Finger on her adult hand, but the Short Index Finger on her childhood hand will always remain that way. This woman knows all about his inner turmoil. She'll see his self-deprecating smile and understand where it comes from. In fact, it may be what first intrigued her about him as he stared into his drink or down at his shoes when they met. Both of these people will be overly sensitive to criticism. This is what they need to come to grips with if they marry, because it's the single factor that can tear at their wonderful bond. Harville Hendrix wrote a sensitive and thoughtful book called *Getting the Love You Want* that I recommend to all of my clients. It gives you a clear understanding of why you are in the relationship you are and how to make it the best it can be.

Men who were born shy can also make a successful marriage with a woman who has Average Index Fingers, though she won't have any clear idea of why he reacts the way he does unless she reads this book. It's just not easy for a person who was born with confidence to put themselves into the shoes of a shy person. If the rest of the hands are compatible, there is no reason why a shy man can't find refuge with the strengths of an easygoing partner, as long as she respects him and lets him know how much she loves and values him. I cannot emphasize enough that, no matter what the character of two people who fall in love, basic respect for your partner is paramount. It takes patience to hold your tongue and think things through when anger erupts. But what a payoff there can be, keeping his love and his devotion only for you.

A FINAL NOTE

Looking at a man's life by analyzing his hands tells you things he cannot speak about and may not even recall. For as long as I have been reading hands I still get a thrill each time someone holds theirs out and lets me see into their private world. In every case I feel excited to tell them what is there, where they came from and how far they've journeyed.

This book, with *The Love Deck* as an easy guide, gives you a new way to look at your man. You may be in a marriage of many years with established patterns of behavior. How do you go about changing these when it's human nature to fear change? You may have recognized yourself and your man in these pages and felt relief to understand why you relate to each other the way you do. That is your starting point. There is no blame to be placed on either of you, only new foundations to be laid.

Love and anger are closely tied. One can turn into the other in a split second, depending on what is said or even what is inferred. What you've learned about your man should help to change your response when a squabble breaks out. Put yourself in his shoes. Reading his hands has given you the keys to his deepest vulnerabilities. You are now the keeper of his secrets. Use them to decipher his signals, even the silences. You will be surprised to find that when you respond to him with warmth and compassion and real understanding, his anger melts and love grows in its place.

ACKNOWLEDGMENTS

Without the support of so many people, this book could not have been written. My parents, Jean and Gord, encouraged my curiosity and independence and showed me that love is the only thing that counts. My daughter, Sophie, is and always has been the wind beneath my wings. For insightful critiques, stimulating viewpoints and technical expertise, I have my very special siblings, Jeanette, Sitara and Bruce.

Years of wandering the world did not diminish the bond between true friends who shared every aspect of their lives and countless memorable meals; Billie Stone, Linda Stork, Barneita and Albert Running, Caroline Keenan, B.J. Matthews, David Jones, Maayken and her dear Ryan Earl, Alex St Germain, Vickie and Ross Dawe, Jordy Stone, Dorothy Botting, John Martins Manteiga and David Poole. Janice Isomura and Ken Evoy gave invaluable encouragement. Lisa Hagan always had a kind word.

Professional admiration for talented hand readers Nathaniel Altman and Judith Hipskind-Collins turned into lifelong friendships that I cherish. The great writers Colin Wilson and Jeffrey Moussaieff-Masson gave moral support and advice while I toiled over the manuscript. Final gratitude goes to my stalwart literary agent, June Clark, who shepherded this project into the hands of my gifted editor at Running Press, Jennifer Kasius.